THE

RULES

OF

MANAGEMENT

THE

RULES

OF

MANAGEMENT

A Irreverent Guide for the
Leader, Innovator, Diplomat,
Politician, Therapist, Warrior,
and Saint in Everyone

RICHARD TEMPLAR

PEARSON
Prentice
Hall

Library of Congress Publication Number: 2004116371

Publisher: Tim Moore
Acquisitions Editor: Paula Sinnott
Editorial Assistant: Kate Stephenson
International Marketing Manager: Tim Galligan
Cover Designer: Sandra Schroeder
Managing Editor: Gina Kanouse
Senior Project Editor: Lori Lyons
Copy Editor: Keith Cline
Compositor: Karen Kennedy, Jake McFarland
Manufacturing Buyer: Dan Uhrig

© 2005 by Pearson Education, Inc.
Publishing as Prentice Hall
Upper Saddle River, New Jersey 07458

Prentice Hall offers excellent discounts on this book when ordered in quantity for bulk purchases or special sales. For more information, please contact U.S. Corporate and Government Sales, 1-800-382-3419, corpsales@pearsontechgroup.com. For sales outside the U.S., please contact International Sales, 1-317-581-3793, international@pearsontech-group.com.

Printed in the United States of America

First Printing June, 2005

ISBN 0-13-187036-X

Pearson Education LTD.
Pearson Education Australia PTY, Limited.
Pearson Education Singapore, Pte. Ltd.
Pearson Education North Asia, Ltd.
Pearson Education Canada, Ltd.
Pearson Educatión de Mexico, S.A. de C.V.
Pearson Education—Japan
Pearson Education Malaysia, Pte. Ltd.

Contents

CONTENTS

CONTENTS

CONTENTS

CONTENTS

Introduction

Strange thing, management. It's something few of us set out in life to do, yet most of us find ourselves doing at some point.

Career adviser:	What would you like to do when you finish school?
16-year-old:	I want to be a manager.

Did this happen to you? No, me neither. But here you are anyway.

As a manager you are expected to be a lot of things. A tower of strength, a leader and innovator, a magician (conjuring up pay raises, resources, and extra staff at the drop of a hat), a kindly uncle/aunt, a shoulder to cry on, a dynamic motivator, a stern but fair judge, a diplomat, a politician, a financial wizard (no, this is quite different from being a magician), a protector, a savior and a saint.

You are responsible for a whole group of people who you probably didn't pick, may not like, might have nothing in common with, and who perhaps won't like you much. You have to coax out of them a decent day's work. You are also responsible for their physical, emotional, and mental safety and care. You have to make sure they don't hurt themselves—or each other. You have to ensure they can carry out their jobs according to whatever guidelines your industry warrants. You have to know your rights, their rights, the company's rights, the union's rights.

And on top of all this, you're expected to do your job as well.

Oh yes, and you have to remain cool and calm—you can't shout, throw things, or have favorites. This management business is a tall order....

You are responsible for looking after and getting the best out of a team. This team may behave at times like young children—and

> ## "YOU ARE RESPONSIBLE FOR A WHOLE GROUP OF PEOPLE WHO YOU PROBABLY DIDN'T PICK, MAY NOT LIKE, MIGHT HAVE NOTHING IN COMMON WITH, AND WHO PERHAPS WON'T LIKE YOU MUCH."

you can't smack them* (or possibly even fire them). At other times they will behave like petulant teenagers—sleeping in late, not showing up, refusing to do any real work if they do show up, skipping out early—that sort of thing.

Like you, I've managed teams (in my case, up to a hundred people at a time). People whose names I was expected to know, and all their little foibles—ah, Heather can't work late on Tuesday because her daughter has to be picked up from play group. Trevor is colorblind, so we can't use him at the trade show. Mandy sulks

---

* Yes, yes, I know you can't smack children either. I was just making a point. Please don't write in.

> "AS A MANAGER, YOU ARE ALSO EXPECTED TO BE A BUFFER ZONE BETWEEN HIGHER MANAGEMENT AND YOUR STAFF."

if left to answer the phones at lunchtime and loses us customers. Chris is great in a team but can't motivate herself to do anything solo. Ray drinks and shouldn't be allowed to drive himself anywhere.

As a manager, you are also expected to be a buffer zone between higher management and your staff. Nonsense may come down from on high, but you have to a) sell it to your team, b) not groan loudly or laugh, and c) get your team to work with it even if it is nonsense.

You also have to justify the "no pay raises this year" mentality even if it has just completely demotivated your team. You will have to keep secret any knowledge you have of takeovers, mergers, acquisitions, secret deals, senior management buyouts, and the like, despite the fact that rumors are flying and you are being constantly asked questions by your team.

You are responsible not only for people but also for budgets, discipline, communications, efficiency, legal matters, union matters, health and safety matters, personnel matters, pensions, sick pay, maternity leave, paternity leave, holidays, time off, time out, time sheets, charity collections, schedules, industry standards, fire drills, first aid, fresh air, heating, plumbing, parking spaces, lighting, stationery, resources, and coffee. And that's not to mention the small matter of customers.

And you will have to fight with other departments, other teams, clients, senior bosses, senior management, the board, shareholders, and the accounting department (unless, of course, you are the manager of the accounting department).

You are also expected to set standards. This means you are going to have to be an on-time, up-front, smartly dressed, hardworking, industrious, late-staying, early-rising, detached, responsible, caring, knowledgeable, above-reproach juggler. Tall order.

You also need to accept that as a manager you may be ridiculed, derided as a manipulative obstructionist pen pusher and possibly even judged by your staff, shareholders, and/or the public to be ineffective and even superfluous to the carrying out of the actual job at hand.*

And all you wanted to do was your job . . . . Luckily there are a few hints and tips that will have you sailing through it looking cool, earning points, and coming out smelling like roses. These are *The Rules of Management*—the unwritten, unspoken, unacknowledged Rules. Keep them to yourself if you want to stay one step ahead of the game.

Management is an art and a science. There are textbooks of thousands of pages devoted to how to do it. There are countless training courses. (You've probably been in a few.) However, what

---

* If this all makes you feel a bit down about being a manager—don't be. Managers are the stuff that runs the world. We get to lead, to inspire, to motivate, to guide, to shape the future. We get to make a difference to the business and to people's lives. We get to make a real and positive contribution to the state of the world. We get, not only, to be part of the solution, but to provide the solution itself. We are the sheriff and the marshal and the ranger all rolled into one. We are the engine and the captain. It's a great role, and we should relish it—it's just not always an easy role.

"AND ALL YOU WANTED
TO DO WAS YOUR JOB."

no textbook contains and no training course includes are the various "unwritten" rules that make you a good, effective, and decent manager. *The Rules of Management.* Whether you are responsible for only one or two people or thousands—it doesn't matter. The Rules are the same.

You won't find anything here you probably didn't already know. Or if you didn't know it, then you will read it and say, "But that's really obvious." Yes, it is all really obvious, if you think hard enough about it. But in the fast-paced, frantic, just-about-coping kind of life we lead, you may not have thought about it lately. And what isn't so obvious is whether or not you do it.

It's just fine to say "But I know that already." Yes, as a smart person you probably do, but ask yourself honestly for each rule: Do you put it into practice, carry it out, work with it as standard? Are you sure?

I've arranged these Rules for you into two sections:

* Managing your team
* Managing you

I think that should be fairly simple. The Rules aren't arranged in any particular order of importance—the first ones aren't more important than later ones or vice versa. Read them all and then start to put them into practice, adopting the ones that seem easiest to you first. A lot of them will flow together so that you can begin to carry them out simultaneously, unconsciously. Soon we'll have you looking cool and relaxed, confident and assertive, in charge,

> "SOON WE'LL HAVE YOU LOOKING COOL AND RELAXED, CONFIDENT AND ASSERTIVE, IN CHARGE, IN CONTROL, ON TOP OF THINGS, AND MANAGING MARVELOUSLY."

in control, on top of things, and managing marvelously. Not bad considering it wasn't too long ago you were shoulder to the wheel, nose to the grindstone, ear to the ground, and back to the wall. Well done, you.

Before we begin, it might be worth taking a moment or two to determine what exactly we all mean by "management." And that isn't as easy as it sounds. For my money we are all managers—parents,* the self-employed, the entrepreneur, the employed, even the ones who inherited wealth. We all have to "manage." It might only be ourselves, but we still have to cope, to make the best use of resources available, motivate, plan, process, facilitate,

---

* If you don't believe parents have to be managers too, then read Ros Jay's *Kids & Co: Winning Business Tactics for Every Family*, White Ladder Press, 2003.

monitor, measure success, set standards, budget, execute, and work. It's just that some of us have to do all that with bigger teams. But the fundamental stuff doesn't change.

The Harvard Business School defines a manager as someone who "gets results through other people." The great management consultant Peter Drucker says a manager is someone who has the responsibility to plan, execute, and monitor; while the Australian Institute of Management definition of a manager is a person who "plans, leads, organizes, delegates, controls, evaluates, and budgets in order to achieve an outcome." I can go along with that.

It can get very wordy and complex:

> A manager is an employee who forms part of the organization's management team and is accountable for exercising delegated authority over human, financial, and material management to accomplish the objectives of the organization. Managers are responsible for managing human resources, communicating, practicing and promoting the corporate values, ethics, and culture of the organization, and for leading and managing change within the organization. (The Leadership Network, California)

Fine, whatever. We are all managers in whatever form or shape we think and we all have to get to with the job of managing. Anything that makes our life simpler is a bonus. Here are the simple *Rules of Management*. They aren't devious or underhanded. Actually they are all pretty obvious. But if you think about each carefully and implement each without fail, you'll be amazed what a difference it will make to your work and your life.

You may *know* everything in this book, but do you *do* it? This book will help motivate you into doing what you already know.

Let's get started . . . .

PART 1

MANAGING

YOUR TEAM

We all have to work with people. These may be loosely known as a team, department, squad, crew—even a posse. It doesn't matter. The mistake a lot of managers make is to think they are managing people. They think that people are their tools. Make the people successful and you have the successful manager—or so the theory goes.

But unfortunately this is a myth, and we need to see that the real role of the manager is to manage processes rather than people. People can manage themselves if you let them. What you need to be concentrating on is the real job of management—the strategy. The team is merely a means to fulfilling that end. If all your people could be replaced by machines—and how many of us haven't prayed that this might happen?—we would still need a strategy, still manage the process.

The people may have disappeared and been replaced by automatons, but the real job would still be there. The good manager is managing change, process, strategy, progress, and balance. In all of this we might need our "people," but we also may not. We can't ignore the people, of course, but we should be handing over as much self-management to them as we possibly can.

> "PEOPLE CAN MANAGE THEMSELVES IF YOU LET THEM."

> "WHAT YOU NEED TO BE
> CONCENTRATING ON IS
> THE REAL JOB OF
> MANAGEMENT—THE
> STRATEGY."

Of course we, as managers, have to work with real flesh-and-blood people and we have to know what motivates them, how they think and feel, why they come to work, why they give their best (or their worst), what they are afraid of, and their hopes and dreams. We have to encourage them, coach them, give them the resources to do their job and manage themselves, oversee their processes, and set their strategy for them. We will worry about them, look out for them, be on their side and support them. But we won't manage them. We will let them manage themselves while we concentrate on our real role as a manager.

RULE 1

Get Them Emotionally Involved

"Work for something because it is good, not just because it stands a chance to succeed."

Vaclav Havel, President of the Czech Republic

You manage people. People who are paid to do a job. But if it is "just a job" to them, you'll never get their best. If they come to work looking to clock in and clock out and do as little as they can get away with in between, then you're doomed to failure, my friend. On the other hand, if they come to work looking to enjoy themselves, looking to be stretched, challenged, inspired, and to get involved, then you have a big chance of getting the very best out of them. Trouble is, the jump from drudge to super team is entirely up to you. It is *you* who has to inspire them, lead them, motivate them, challenge them, get them emotionally involved.

That's okay. You like a challenge yourself, don't you? The good news is that getting a team emotionally involved is easy. All you have to do is make them care about what they are doing. And that's easy too. You have to get them to see the relevance of what they are doing, how it makes an impact on people's lives, how they provide for the needs of other human beings, how they can reach out and touch people by what they do at work. Get them convinced—because it is true—that what they do makes a difference, that it contributes to society in some way other than filling the owner's or shareholders' pockets, or ensures that the chief executive gets a big fat paycheck.

And yes, I know it's easier to show how they contribute if you manage nurses rather than an advertising sales team, but if you think about it, then you can find value in any role and instill pride in those who do whatever job it is. Prove it? Okay. Well, those who sell advertising space are helping other companies, some of which may be very small, reach their markets. They are alerting potential customers to things they may have wanted for a long time and may really need. They are keeping the newspaper or magazine afloat because it relies on ad sales income, and that magazine or newspaper delivers information and/or gives pleasure to the people who buy it (otherwise they wouldn't, would they?).

Get them to care because that's an easy thing to do. Look, this is a given. Everyone deep down wants to be valued and to be useful. The cynics will say this is nonsense, but it is true, deep down true. All you have to do is reach down far enough and you will find feeling, concern, responsibility, and involvement. Drag all that stuff up and they'll follow you forever and not even realize why.

Oh, just make sure that you've convinced yourself first before you try this out on your team. Do you believe that what you do makes a positive difference? If you're not sure, reach down, deep down, and find a way to care.

> "GET THEM CONVINCED—
> BECAUSE IT IS TRUE—
> THAT WHAT THEY DO
> MAKES A DIFFERENCE."

RULE 2

Know What a Team Is and How It Works

"Gettin' good players is easy. Gettin' 'em to play together is the hard part."

Casey Stengel, former manager, New York Yankees

So what is a team and how does it operate? If we are going to be successful managers, we have to know the answers to these questions.

A team isn't a collection of people. It is an organization with its own dynamics, qualities, and conventions. Without knowing these things you will flounder. Knowing them, you can work your team to achieve greatness.

In every team there are a variety of people all pushing and shoving in different directions and with unequal force. Some shove louder, if you know what I mean. Others are happy to push from the back. Others don't appear to be doing anything, but you'll need them for ideas.

If you haven't looked at team dynamics before, I urge you to read Meredith Belbin's *Management Teams: Why They Succeed or Fail*.*(If you have, pass right on to the next Rule.) This is designed for managers concerned with achieving results by getting the best from their key people. I'll paraphrase what he says, but I do urge you to practice what he preaches.

---

* R. Meredith Belbin, *Management Teams: Why They Succeed or Fail*, Butterworth-Heinemann, 2nd edition 2003.

Belbin says that there are nine team roles—and we all carry out one or more functions of these team roles. Yes, it is fun to identify our own, but it is much more useful to identify your team's and then work with that information.

The nine team roles are as follows:

- The Plant—They are original thinkers; they generate new ideas; they offer solutions to problems; they think in radically different ways, laterally, imaginatively.

- The Resource Investigator—They are creative; they like to take ideas and run with them; they are extroverted and popular.

- The Coordinator—They are highly disciplined and controlled; they can focus on objectives; they unify a team.

- The Shaper—They are very achievement orientated; they like to be challenged and to get results.

- The Monitor Evaluator—They analyze and balance and weigh; they are calm and detached; they are objective thinkers.

- The Team Worker—They are supportive and cooperative; they make good diplomats because they only want what is best for the team.

- The Implementer—They have good organizational skills; they display common sense; they like to get the job done.

- The Completer—They check details; they tidy up after themselves; they are painstakingly conscientious.

- The Specialist—They are dedicated to acquiring a specialized skill; they are extremely professional; they have drive and dedication.

Now you know who you might have in your team. So what exactly is a team and how are you going to make yours more effective? Again, read Belbin and also come to understand a team is a group where all the members focus on a collective target. A team doesn't come together well when each individual member focuses on their own target—be that just getting to the end of the day, their own personal progress, how to betray the boss (that's you, by the way), use work as a social club, and so on.

> ## "A TEAM DOESN'T COME TOGETHER WELL WHEN EACH INDIVIDUAL MEMBER FOCUSES ON THEIR OWN TARGET."

You'll know you have a team when you hear "we" and "us" more often than "I" and "me."

You'll know you have a team when difficult decisions become easy—because someone says, "It's okay, we're all in this together."

You'll know you have a team when the team tells you it is a team.

Set Realistic Targets —No, Really Realistic

"Let's make a dent in the universe."

Steve Jobs, CEO, Apple

When I was doing research for this book, someone said that setting realistic targets was unrealistic and that all targets should be "stretching" ones because that would impress the board. Now, can you see the problem here? Yep, we're not talking about motivating a team, getting a job done, creating an atmosphere of success and creativity. No, we're talking about impressing the board. Now on paper that might be a smart thing to do if your board is made up of monkeys, but I bet it isn't. I bet it's made up of pretty shrewd cookies who would see through a maneuver like that in a nanosecond.

When I say realistic, I don't say lower or easy-to-achieve targets. I say realistic. That might mean taxing. It might mean a struggle. It might mean your team has to redouble its efforts, work harder, longer, smarter. But Rule 3 says realistic, and that means achievable, within your grasp. And yes, you might have to stretch a bit.

Realistic means you know what your team is capable of and what is expected by your bosses. Somehow you will have to marry the two to keep both sides happy. You can't pressure your team out of existence, nor can you let your bosses think you're lazy.

If your bosses insist on setting targets that aren't realistic, you must feed that back to them. Don't argue or procrastinate; feed it back to them. Ask how they think the targets could be achieved.

RULE 3

Say they are unrealistic. Be very well prepared, make your case that the targets are unrealistic and ask again how they think they could be achieved. Suggest a realistic target of your own, well supported by facts and figures. Keep feeding the problem back to your bosses and asking for clarification. Sooner or later they must set a more realistic target or order you to achieve the impossible. Either way, you are resolved of the problem. If they set you realistic targets, then all you need to do is meet them. (You know you can do this.) If they order you to fulfill unrealistic ones, you are also in the clear; when you fail to achieve the unachievable you will be able to explain that at the time you did register your protest and bring your case back to them.

> "KEEP FEEDING THE
> PROBLEM BACK TO YOUR
> BOSSES."

Hold Effective Meetings —No, Really Effective

"The ideas that come out of most brainstorming sessions are usually superficial, trivial, and not very original. They are rarely useful. The process, however, seems to make uncreative people feel that they are making innovative contributions and that others are listening to them."

A. Harvey Block, CEO, Bokenon Systems

We've all been to them—the meetings that drag on, people who ramble, agendas written on the back of an envelope or spur of the moment, any-other-business surprises, lack of information, insufficient notice.

As a manager you will have to hold meetings. Make them effective. Decide in advance what the objective of the meeting is and make sure you meet that objective.

Basically, meetings only have four purposes:

* To create and fuse a team
* To impart information
* To brainstorm ideas (and make decisions)
* To collect information (and make decisions)

Some meetings might cover one or more of these, but you should still be aware of that and add it into your objective. If your meeting is to impart information, then do it and get the heck out. If it's a discussion about that information you want, then that's a

> ## "DECIDE IN ADVANCE WHAT THE OBJECTIVE OF THE MEETING IS AND MAKE SURE YOU MEET THAT OBJECTIVE."

different type of meeting and as such should have different objectives. Be aware that some meetings are there to help your team meet each other, bond, socialize together, find out about each other, and see you in your true role as the team leader.

If you want your meetings to be effective, then remain firmly in control—no wishy-washy democracies here. You are the manager and you are in charge—end of story. To be effective you shouldn't allow anyone to reminisce, ramble, refuse to be quiet, or relax. Keep 'em moving fast and get them out the door as soon as you can.

You don't do "any other business"—ever. If it's important it should be on the agenda. If it isn't, then it shouldn't be there at all. "Any other business" is invariably someone trying to put something over on someone else. Don't allow it—ever.

Hold all meetings at the end of the day rather than at the beginning. Everyone's anxious to leave for home and it keeps meetings shorter; at the beginning of the day everyone has plenty of time to digress and chat. Of course, if it is a bonding meeting, you can hold it at the beginning of the day.

See how many meetings you could hold by e-mail, phone, one to one. (Cut out everyone who isn't absolutely essential.)

Start all meetings on time. Never wait for anyone. Never go back over stuff for latecomers. If they've missed something vital, they can get it from others after the meeting and it'll learn 'em to be on time next time.* Useful tip—never schedule meetings to begin exactly on the hour, always say 3:10 rather than 3 o'clock. You'll find people will always be more punctual if you set an "odd" time. Try 3:35 if you want to be really wacky.

Schedule the meeting far enough in advance—but not too far—so that no one can say they had something else scheduled. Confirm the day before with everyone to make sure they have remembered and can make it.

> ## "START ALL MEETINGS ON TIME. NEVER WAIT FOR ANYONE."

---

* The Toad, having finished his breakfast, picked up a stout stick and swung it vigorously, belabouring imaginary animals. 'I'll learn 'em to steal my house!' he cried. 'I'll learn 'em, I'll learn 'em!' 'Don't say "learn 'em," Toad,' said the Rat, greatly shocked. 'It's not good English.' 'What are you always nagging at Toad for?' inquired the Badger, rather peevishly. 'What's the matter with his English? It's the same what I use myself, and if it's good enough for me, it ought to be good enough for you!' 'I'm very sorry,' said the Rat humbly. 'Only I THINK it ought to be "teach 'em", not "learn 'em."' 'But we don't WANT to teach 'em,' replied the Badger. 'We want to LEARN 'em – learn 'em, learn 'em! And what's more, we're going to DO it, too!' (Kenneth Grahame, *The Wind in the Willows*)

RULE 4

You decide who keeps the minutes— and make sure they do, and to your satisfaction. You don't have to be bossy or aggressive about this, just firm, friendly, and utterly in control.

Make sure every point on the agenda ends up with an action plan —no action plan means it was just a chat. Or a decision, of course.

If meetings are getting too big—more than six people—start to subdivide them into committees and get your committees to report back.

And most important of all—engrave this one on your heart—all meetings must have a definite purpose. At the end of the meeting, you must be able to say whether or not you met that purpose. Oh yes, and hold all meetings on uncomfortable chairs (or standing, à la *West Wing*)—that speeds things up considerably.

Make Meetings Fun

"Don't tell me you lost your sense of humor already?"

Roger Rabbit in *Who Framed Roger Rabbit?*

I guess that when you were working your way up to your illustrious position of today you had to sit through many interminable meetings, all boring, all stupifyingly dull. Well, the pattern has to be broken somewhere, and I'm relying on you to break it. The old ways of doing meetings has to stop, and you're the very person to do it.

So let's make 'em fun. Now, before we go on, I remember a tip I read somewhere. Basically you were supposed to give out five coins to each meeting member and when they wanted to speak they had to spend a penny. Once they had used up their coins they were done and couldn't say anything more. It was supposed to make people really cautious about speaking and reluctant to

> "THE OLD WAYS OF DOING MEETINGS HAS TO STOP, AND YOU'RE THE VERY PERSON TO DO THE STOPPING."

RULE 5

spend all their coins on trivial topics. Fun? Maybe. But it would also get you quite a reputation as a fool and/or an ineffectual meeting leader—as would other suggestions, such as the following:

- Costumes
- Food and/or drink (unless it's lunchtime, in which case that's functional, not fun; or if you take your team out to a restaurant or to a bar, and then it's not a meeting, it's a bonding session— or a thank you, of course: *see* Rule 17)
- Games, quizzes, or contests of any type
- Having small surprises such as chocolates hidden under the chairs
- A talking stick (don't ask—a New Age Californian thing)
- Blindfolds
- Letting the most junior member chair the meeting.

All of these head toward farce, ruin, and idiocy. Don't go there.

So how can you lighten things up without looking like a fool? Well, for a start fun doesn't have to mean silly or stupid or unfunny.

Fun means not being stuffy, allowing people to be themselves and to bring their own contribution. Fun means allowing people to share things that have made them laugh without being frowned on. Fun is about letting people tell stories or anecdotes that lighten the mood. (Just know when to say, "Okay, back to work.") Fun means being flexible enough to allow other suggestions as to where and how you all meet. Perhaps your organization has a great boardroom—could you meet there? Or outside if the weather is good.

The confident manager—that's you—can be flexible because they are relaxed and cool and confident. The stuffy manager is frightened because they feel insecure and seek a rigid approach to prop up their lack of self-confidence.

Make Your Team Better Than You

"It is one of the strange ironies of this strange life [that] those who work the hardest, who subject themselves to the strictest discipline, who give up certain pleasurable things in order to achieve a goal, are the happiest people."

Brutus Hamilton, decathlon coach

A really good manager, yep that's you again, knows that when their team takes wing and soars, they too will soar. Getting your team to soar takes courage, grit, determination, and an overwhelming passion. You have to make members of your team better than you, which means trusting them, getting them the best resources, training them to take over from you, trusting them not to stab you in the back when it's time to take over from you, and being confident enough in your own abilities not to be jealous of them when they do take off. Not easy.

It takes quite some manager to carry this one out. You have to be pretty relaxed and secure in your own position. Encouraging your team to bring it on takes guts, quite frankly. Let's take a look at your team. Who've you got there? Which ones will one day fill your shoes? What can you share with them to bring them on?

Shoe-fillers are the ones you want to cultivate and grow. They are the bright ones, the keen ones, the eager beavers. I once had a young assistant who was so sharp he scared me. But when I did move on up, he filled my shoes. And he came with me over several moves, always one step behind. Now the crazy thing was he was better than me in lots of ways but he never chanced his arm and overtook me. It could have been out of respect, but I doubt it—the industry I worked in was a little cutthroat to say the least. No, it was habit. And once you've built a good team, it gets in the habit of having you as the manager and then it feels comfortable with that and doesn't overtake you. Teams only do that when they feel resentful or mistrusted. So bring 'em on and train 'em and make 'em better.

> ## "ONCE YOU'VE BUILT A GOOD TEAM, IT GETS IN THE HABIT OF HAVING YOU AS THE MANAGER."

Set Your Boundaries

"It is unfortunate we can't buy many business executives for what they are worth and sell them for what they think they are worth."

Malcolm Forbes, American publisher

You have to, right from day one, be totally on top of the discipline issue. Remember earlier we talked about how looking after your team can be a bit like being a parent? Well, as a parent you pretty much have to set boundaries and practice zero tolerance to survive. Give 'em an inch and they'll take a mile. If you are seen to be "soft," they'll take advantage. The good thing with clear boundaries and zero tolerance is you have a finite line—a yardstick by which you can judge everything. All you have to do is ask, "Is this a breach of the rules?" If it is, stop it. If you do allow it, where do you stop?

"THE GOOD THING WITH ZERO TOLERANCE IS YOU HAVE A FINITE LINE—A YARDSTICK BY WHICH YOU CAN JUDGE EVERYTHING."

Say one of your clear boundaries is tracking work hours. (It might be dress or customer care or whatever, but just say it's tracking work hours.) If one minute late is fine, what about two? If two is fine, what about three? And so on until people are wandering in at whatever time they feel like. But if you don't allow it, then that's the end of the story. You don't have to think about that particular issue any more. Whereas if you do allow infringements, small breaches, you are forever having to consider, "Is this a step too far?" "Can I gain control back?" "How far am I prepared to go?"

This doesn't mean you need to have hundreds of rules and be ridiculously inflexible. It means that you need to decide on your few key boundaries that are important to you and to the team and the business. Make them clear. And make them firm.

Remember you are dealing with a team—I will stress this again and again throughout this book—and not an individual. You might feel that for each and every person an exception can be made, but you aren't dealing with individuals—you are dealing with a team. If you are seen to be soft on one individual, then you must be soft on everyone. If you allow one to wander in late, then everyone must be allowed to wander in late. If one person can get away with breaking the rules, then everyone must be allowed.

The good manager is firm on inappropriate behavior because this sends out a clear message to the team—the message that you are a good, firm, in-control sort of manager who values what the team can achieve collectively rather than a reputation as an easy-going, laid-back, nice person. Yes, individually some of the team may rate you as pretty cool if you let them get away with murder, but the team will collectively disdain you.

Be Ready to Cut

"No one can whistle a symphony. It takes an orchestra to play it."

H. E. Luccock, Christian preacher

Okay, so you've got your orchestra and you get them to play. You listen. Something's wrong somewhere. Yep, that flute player is out of tune, off key, and playing from a different hymn sheet. Now you have three choices:

* Put up with it
* Change it
* End it

Let's have a little look at these three because, as in all things— from relationships, to life, to work, to being a parent—these three choices are the same every single time.

So, you're going to put up with it. This makes your entire orchestra sound flat, out of tune, and ill-fitted to do its job properly—that of supplying sweet music to the masses. Your listening public (your objective) will not listen and will accuse you, the orchestra leader, of being a nincompoop*—and they would be right.

Okay, so you're going to try to change it. Flute player X gets some retraining. They get sent to a remedial flute course. They come back with the right hymn sheet but have decided to switch

---

* They don't of course use this word, but I'm not allowed to use the word they really would use.

to the bassoon because they were feeling creatively hemmed in by the flute. Problem solved. Well done for tackling it.

However, what if their report says they are tone deaf and should never have been in the orchestra in the first place and should have taken up a career sounding the fire alarm somewhere? What you can't do is then embark on another course of action where you give them the triangle to play but they mess that up too and by now the rest of the orchestra has lost confidence in you and is beginning a mutiny.

Time for the third course. You fire them. It is swift and kind. They can then go on to become a champion alarm ringer somewhere—somewhere else that is—and your orchestra recognizes you as decisive, knowing what you want, objective (you put the need of the many before the bad playing of one), and utterly in charge. Give yourself an extra brownie point.

Always be ready to cut the dead wood, straggly growth, lousy flute players (and any other team players who don't cut the mustard).

"ALWAYS BE READY
TO CUT THE
DEAD WOOD."

Offload as Much as You Can—or Dare

"If it feels painful and scary—that's real delegation."

Caspian Woods, *From Acorns—How to Build Your Brilliant Business from Scratch*

The good manager, and that is you from now on, knows that they manage events, processes, situations, and strategies—but never people. Look, let's imagine you have a big garden and decide to employ a gardener. Do you manage the gardener? No. They manage themselves quite nicely, thank you. Your job is to manage the garden. You'll decide what to plant and when and where. The gardener, like a spade or a wheelbarrow, becomes a tool in that garden and a tool you can use to manage your garden effectively. But you don't manage the gardener. They manage themselves. You tell them what you want done, and they do it. You delegate, and they dig and delve and plant and prune and tend and weed. The plants actually manage themselves as well; neither you nor the gardener actually grows anything—you both manage. The gardener is your useful assistant, your tool to getting stuff done.

Now it makes sense to give the gardener as much to do with the decision-making process as possible to free you up for long-term strategy, seeing the big picture, seasonal planning, and perusing seed catalogs while sitting in the shade sipping a cool drink.

There is no point standing over the gardener while they mow lawns, weed beds, prune trees, and the like. It is better to give them the job to do and then let them do it. Once they have finished you can check their work and make sure it is satisfactory. And then you probably won't need to do that again—don't keep checking.

And that basically is the secret of good management. Give 'em a job to do and let them do it. Check once or twice to make sure they've done it the way you want it done, and then next time just let them do it. Increasingly give them more and more to do and stand back more and more from the people processes and concentrate instead on the planning processes. Build your team and then trust them to do their jobs. Sometimes this will backfire and people will fool around, desert the job, do things badly—and hey, that'll be entirely your fault because you are the manager and it's your team. No, that's serious, it is entirely your responsibility. Read on and we'll find ways to make sure it doesn't happen—well, not too often anyway.

> "BUILD YOUR TEAM AND THEN TRUST THEM TO DO THEIR JOBS."

Let Them Make Mistakes

"A boss fixes blame, a manager fixes mistakes."

Anonymous

There is an old Chinese saying that goes something like this: "Tell me and I'll remember for an hour; show me and I'll remember for a day; but let me do it and I'll remember forever." That sounds about right. And if you are going to let people do it, then they are going to do it badly at first. They are going to make mistakes. And you are going to let them.

If you are a parent, you know the agonizing thing you go through with a two-year-old who insists they can pour their own drink—

> "TELL ME AND I'LL
> REMEMBER FOR AN HOUR;
> SHOW ME AND I'LL
> REMEMBER FOR A DAY;
> BUT LET ME DO IT AND
> I'LL REMEMBER FOREVER."

and then proceeds to spill most of it on the table. You stand by with a rag behind your back because you know that

- They are going to spill it.
- You are going to have to mop it up.
- The spilling process is important, and you have to let them do it, and they will progress to not spilling, but only once they have the spilling out of the way first.

As a parent you do that wonderful hovering thing, ready to grab the juice if it is going to spill too much, or grab the cup if it is going over, or even grab the child if he or she is going to fall off the chair due to such intense concentration.

I'm not saying members of your team are like young children— well, I am actually, but don't tell them—but it is imperative you learn to let them do the spilling if they are to progress. Make sure you have your rag behind your back ready to mop up after them.

And after each spilling, you don't scold them. Instead you offer praise— "Well done, brilliant job, incredible progress." Try not to let them see the rag or the mopping up.

Accept Their Limitations

"Making mistakes simply means you are learning faster."

Weston H. Agor, *Intuitive Management*

As we saw earlier, effectively fusing a team together means you need several different parts—or team members. Now some of us are good at certain things and others not so. If we were all the same we wouldn't be able to work as a team—we would all be leaders or all followers, and you need a combination, not either/or.

So if some members of your team aren't leaders—or followers— you have to accept that. If some are good with numbers and others not, you have to accept that. If some are good at working unsupervised and others not, you have to accept that.

> "IF WE WERE ALL THE SAME WE WOULDN'T BE ABLE TO WORK AS A TEAM —WE WOULD ALL BE LEADERS OR ALL FOLLOWERS."

RULE 11

And to be able to accept these things you have to know your staff pretty well. You have to know their strengths and weaknesses, good points and bad. If you don't—and I'm sure this doesn't apply to you—you will be forever trying to shove round pegs into square holes and vice versa.

You have to accept that not everyone is going to be as bright, as determined, as ambitious, as clever, or as motivated as you are— praise indeed from me, but see the next Rule. Some of your team are quite possibly going to be brain dead from the feet up and you might need to practice Rule 8 before Rule 11 if there simply is no hope. But don't act in haste. You might not need a team of geniuses. (In fact if you hire people far too smart for a job, they will just leave fast.)

Suppose your team contains machine operators or admin assistants. Now you don't need these good people to have Einstein brains nor to be really on the ball when it comes to brainstorming. But you do need them to be able to sit in a gluteus-numbing position for hours at a time concentrating on a bit of work that would drive you or me crazy. Just don't go expecting them to take creative wing and soar away with new ideas, new innovations, or new technologies. You have to accept their limitations—and love them for them because these limitations are their parameters by which you can get the very best out of them—their best of course. And while you're at it, have a quick check of your own limitations. What's that? You haven't got any? Come on.

Encourage People

> "A group becomes a team when each member is sure enough of himself and his contribution to praise the skills of the others."

Norman Glass Shidle, *The Art of Successful Communication*

If you don't let people know you're pleased with them, they'll wilt. People come to work for a whole variety of reasons—most, nothing to do with the money despite what they'll tell you—and right there at the top of their unwritten, unspoken, undeclared list will be "Praise from the boss." That's you by the way, the boss.

They might call it "recognition" or "acknowledgement" or "feeling I've done well"—but how do they know? They know because you tell them.

Now you can praise them retroactively, so to speak—wait until they've done well and then tell them they've done well—or you can encourage them in advance—active praise. Tell them they're going to do well before they've done it. Why? Because the chances of them doing well are that much greater if you have praised them in advance. They won't want to let you down, or themselves.

> ## "TELL THEM THEY'RE GOING TO DO WELL BEFORE THEY'VE DONE IT."

RULE 12

Being a manager is a minimalist's dream. You want to build a great team and you want to do it with the smallest output of resources. Praise is free. It is instantly replaceable, doesn't wear out, is invariably 100 percent effective, is incredibly simple to do, and takes no time at all.

So why don't more managers do it? Because it takes self-assurance. You have to be feeling pretty good about yourself to be able to dish out praise in advance. If you doubt yourself, you'll doubt them. If you doubt them, you'll not praise them because you'll be sure they are going to screw up.

It takes nothing except courage to say, "Come on, you can do it. You'll be fine." The more responsibility you give people, the more you trust them, the more you praise them, the more you encourage them, the more they'll give you in return. Praise costs nothing and brings in plenty. Encouragement should be a given.

Encourage an atmosphere where everyone encourages everyone else— "You can do it" should be heard every day all around you. If you're not saying it, chances are your team isn't either. Encourage the good ones to give the less good ones some help. In any good team an air of fostering help should be actively encouraged and praised when it happens. We're all in this together and we sink or swim together.

Be Very, Very Good at Finding the Right People

> "The best executive is one who has sense enough to pick good people to do what he wants done, and self-restraint enough to keep from meddling with them while they do it."
>
> Theodore Roosevelt, U.S. President (1901–9)

You have to be good at finding the right people to fill the right jobs —and then leave them to do it. Okay, I know this is one rule that requires a certain intuitive touch but I'm sure you know the sort of manager I'm talking about. They seem to surround themselves with capable, competent people and then they just seem to sit back and watch them go for gold. You can do that too. It is a special talent, but one you can cultivate. I guess the skill is in both picking the right people *and* letting go—leaving them alone to do their job. You have to have lots of trust to do that; trust in their ability and trust in your own as well.

You have to have a very clear idea of *who* you are looking for to fill a job as much as *what* you are looking for. For instance, you might need a senior account manager—that is *what* you are looking for. But *who*? Team player? Good all rounder? Someone able to make decisions on the run? Someone who can plan ahead? Someone who understands your industry's quirks? Someone who speaks fluent spreadsheets? Someone who can work with an overexcitable union?

I'm sure you get the idea. If you have a clear picture of *who* you need as well as *what* you need, you make the transition to being a

> ## "YOU HAVE TO BE GOOD AT FINDING THE RIGHT PEOPLE TO FILL THE RIGHT JOBS—AND THEN LEAVE THEM TO DO IT."

manager who seems to have an uncanny knack for finding the right people. It's not a knack, of course, but planning, vision, logic, and hard work.

I once made the mistake of being totally seduced by a manager's credentials—I was a general manager seeking to employ a manager—and failing to look hard enough at *who* he was rather than *what* he was. Yes, he had the credentials and was very good at his job. But he wasn't a team player and saw everything as a competition, mainly between him and the other managers. Fine in itself, but it didn't work for me or the other managers, who all wanted to pull together. This was one case where I was not good at finding the right person. I had found the wrong person, and it took a lot to extricate myself. I had only myself to blame because I hadn't thought sufficiently about who I wanted.

If you're not good at this, or think you could improve, invite somebody you respect to sit in on interviews with you to give you another perspective. Find a mentor or coach to help you work out who you really need.

RULE 14

Take the Rap

"The leaders who work most effectively, it seems to me, never say 'I.' And that's not because they have trained themselves not to say 'I.' They don't think 'I.' They think 'we'; they think 'team.' They understand their job to be to make the team function. They accept responsibility and don't sidestep it, but 'we' gets the credit . . . This is what creates trust, what enables you to get the task done."

Peter F. Drucker, *Managing the Nonprofit Organization*

Sorry, but if the team screws up, it is entirely your fault. If the team does well, the credit is all theirs. A good manager will always take the rap. I know it's easy to use your team as an excuse, but it won't wash. You are the leader, the manager, the boss. If it all goes wrong, you have to stand up and take the flack.

> "IT'S EASY TO USE YOUR
> TEAM AS AN EXCUSE, BUT
> IT WON'T WASH."

It is very easy to say, "We didn't meet our targets because . . ." But you have to say, "I didn't meet my targets because . . ." And that "because" has to be followed by "I", never "they."

It is easy to say, "We didn't meet our targets because young Brian accidentally upset Client X and they pulled out leaving us short of our sales." But who put young Brian in charge of such an important client? You. Who organized the sale? You. It has to be you. And your team will die for you if you ask it to, if you take the rap when the going gets tough, believe me. Nothing generates more loyalty than a boss who's prepared to stand up and say, "I take responsibility."

But I also know this is really tough to do. It takes self-confidence, courage, trust (that you won't get fired or disciplined), and a certain maturity.

You might think it will go against you and look as if you are incompetent. Not so. If your boss sees you stand up and say, "We lost the contract and I take responsibility—these are the steps we're taking to make sure it doesn't happen again" they won't see a failure—they will see a future board member.

Give Credit to the Team When It Deserves It

"It is amazing how much you can accomplish if you do not care who gets the credit."

Harry Truman, U.S. President (1945–53)

Just as you must always stand up and take the blame, so too must you always heap praise and credit on your team when things go well. If that fabulous sale to Client X occurs because you happened to stay up all night working on it and then used an old contact from a previous job and then swung it because you happened to know something the competition didn't— then you say, "The team did it."

Taking the blame does generate loads of loyalty, but so too does giving the team the credit. Say it loudly, in public, sincerely, but do say it. And don't do it tongue in cheek with "My team did it," as if you are giving it credit but making sure everyone knows who really was responsible. The implication that it is your team isn't necessary. Everyone knows it is your team so there is no need to mention it, ever. It is okay to say, "It did a great job, it is a fantastic team. I'm incredibly lucky to have it." This implies you had nothing to do with it and yet everyone knows it is your team and you are its leader so the team will love you and everyone else will think you're incredibly humble and self-effacing. Well done.

Again, all this takes courage and a lot of self-confidence, I know. You work hard and it doesn't seem fair to give the credit away. I know that you really want to stand up and shout, "Look, it was me, I did this, all by myself, okay?" But you can't. You see, you didn't do it all by yourself, no matter how much you might believe that. If you are selling, then it is the team that built the product you are selling. Without that team you would have nothing to sell. Tell the team that selling the product was simple because it had done such a good job. It will glow with pride and redouble its efforts.

> "WITHOUT THAT TEAM
> YOU WOULD HAVE
> NOTHING TO SELL."

Get the Best Resources for Your Team

"A clear vision, backed by definite plans, gives you a tremendous feeling of confidence and personal power."

Brian Tracy, personal and business coach

If your team is a tool you use to get greater glory for little ol' you, then the resources your team uses are the tools it needs to carry it —and thus you—onward and upward. Too many managers think that by cutting their team's resources they are earning some sort of brownie points to be stored up—and used in what? Heaven? I don't think so. You have to get the best resources for your team. By depriving the team, you are depriving it of the chance to shine—to propel you to greater glory.

I know of a lot of managers who say, "Oh, they can manage for a few more years with Windows 95." Or "They probably wouldn't know what to do with broadband, I can save some money if I hold off for a bit." I have even heard, "I try to keep a short rein on what they need in case it gets out of hand."

For heaven's sake. Get your team the best, the very, very best, and then let it do its job—which is to make you look good.

If your people need technology—get it for them even if you have to move heaven and earth. If they need more staff, paper stuff, bigger and better machines, higher-quality tools—go get 'em. Whatever it is they need to get their job done slicker, quicker, better, bigger, faster, more productively, cheaper, whatever—go get it. If you have to argue, sweat blood, plead, beg, bust a budget

> ## "GET YOUR TEAM THE BEST, THE VERY, VERY BEST, AND THEN LET IT DO ITS JOB."

or two—do it. Do it now. You simply can't expect them to a) give of their best, or b) be motivated, if you keep them short. They will talk to other people you know: colleagues in the same organization, friends in other organizations. They will know when they are being short-changed and they will resent it, resent you, and work less effectively. In consequence, you will fail to shine. Ipso facto—go get them the best you can.

Celebrate

> "If people are coming to work excited . . . if they're making mistakes freely and fearlessly . . . if they're having fun . . . if they're concentrating on doing things, rather than preparing reports and going to meetings—then somewhere you have leaders."
>
> Robert Townsend, *Further Up the Organization*

I find an excuse every day to reward my staff with a little something—a modest celebration for a result no matter how small, how trivial it seems. If you do the same, you'll have a motivated staff who have a habit of celebrating every success. And that's so important.

And the rewards? Tiny. A box of doughnuts. Extra froth on their cappuccinos. A chance to go outside and sit in the sun.

Sometimes I declare today a special day because we just got such and such a result and then I take them out to lunch, let them take time off, let them tell me their worst jokes—never all at the same time, however.

And, occasionally, I declare such a special day even if we fail to win an order. I reward mistakes, screw-ups, failures, accidents. Why? Well, they've all worked their butts off, done their best, given their all, and sweated blood. Why shouldn't I reward them? Just because we failed doesn't mean we didn't strive. I am rewarding the effort. I am celebrating all that we did right—effort, struggle, determination, teamwork, drive, and good honest hard work.

> "WHY SHOULDN'T I REWARD THEM? JUST BECAUSE WE FAILED DOESN'T MEAN WE DIDN'T STRIVE."

Don't just celebrate the big wins, celebrate all the little ones as well—obviously with smaller celebrations, but celebrations of some sort nevertheless. Hey, any excuse to go and get a coffee. And a bag of doughnuts (or apples if they like). What does that cost you? Very little, but the warm feeling it generates far exceeds any cost.

Keep Track of Everything You Do and Say

"Watch your thoughts; they become words.
Watch your words; they become actions.
Watch your actions; they become habits.
Watch your habits; they become character.
Watch your character; it becomes your destiny."

Frank Outlaw

Now why would you want to do this, unless you're up to no good? No, quite the reverse in fact. The better a manager you are, the more information you need to keep. Why? Two reasons.

First, consistency. You need to keep everything because you will need to check back from time to time. The question, "Now how did I do this before?" will crop up constantly. Your team needs you to be consistent and you can't be that if you don't remember what you did last time. If Jim won that big contract last time and you gave him a sumptuous lunch and then Terri pulls off a similar deal and you take her out for coffee and a bagel, chances are she's not going to be happy and next time won't give you her very best. So write it down and check back. Similarly if you tell Client X that they are getting the same deal as Client Y, and then they discover that's not true, they will probably take their business elsewhere. Be consistent.

Second, proof. Being a good manager, a damn good manager, may open you up to jealousy, resentment, and distrust. Not everybody is as upfront as you. If your team is giving you 110 percent and someone else's is only giving them 60 percent because they are a bad manager, the chances are they will think you're up to something rather than looking at their own poor mismanagement skills. It just might be useful to be able to show where successful projects orgininated, or that you did everything you said you would.

Decisions have to be taken, memos sent, e-mails written, reports presented. Just keep a record of everything. All e-mails should be saved: This is no big deal because computer storage is so immense these days that if all e-mails ever sent were saved it would still only fill a cyber eggcup.

> "THE BETTER A MANAGER YOU ARE, THE MORE INFORMATION YOU NEED TO KEEP."

Be Sensitive to Friction

"My job is secure. No one else wants it."

Bumper sticker

When you are running a team, you are dealing with people. And sometimes they just decide to aggravate one another. Why? Who knows. They just do. They encroach on each other's space, steal each other's cookies, take each other's parking spaces. Who starts it? Who knows. Can you let it go on? The hell you can. It has to be nipped in the bud. You have to be sensitive to friction almost before it begins—and do something about it. There is no point letting it go on for a day longer than it needs to. But to do this you really do need to be on the ball. You have to know your team very well indeed to spot those first early warning signs.

If you don't nip it in the bud, it will grow into a monster. From tiny nit-picking you'll end up with full-scale war, with the rest of the team taking sides.

What to look out for? Silences when there shouldn't be. Odd complaints, "God, I wish Clare would stop complaining to me so much." Grumblings and bitchy gossip. Fierce competitiveness where there doesn't need to be any. Sudden appearance of demarcation lines, such as potted plants to screen desks. Books or computers on desks being used to screen or shield people. People being left out of social situations. People being left out of office humor.

I'm sure you know as much about this as I do and keep your eyes open and your ear to the ground. The secret is stopping it before it gets too bad. Here you have to be diplomat, parent, politician, and referee. You mustn't be seen to be taking sides. You must be seen as taking swift and resolute action, making it clear that

RULE 19

feuding won't be tolerated. Call them in. Reason with them. Separate them. Swap their shifts. Keep them apart. Make them work together as a partnership. There are a whole slew of things you can do, and I'm sure you'll pick the right one at the right time for the right situation.

> "YOU MUSTN'T BE SEEN TO BE TAKING SIDES. YOU MUST BE SEEN AS TAKING SWIFT AND RESOLUTE ACTION."

Create a Good Atmosphere

"Courtesies of a small and trivial character are the ones which strike deepest in the grateful and appreciating heart."

Henry Clay, nineteenth-century American politician

Creating a good atmosphere isn't only easy but also essential. If your staff are sullen and despondent and depressed and surly—it shows. It shows in their work, the way they handle customers and peers, the way they relate to each other, and most importantly, the way they work with you and for you.

It takes nothing to say good morning politely and mean it. It isn't a chore to make sure everyone has a coffee or tea for a meeting. It takes a second to ask, "How are you today?" The three rules for any workplace are as follows:

* Politeness
* Friendliness
* Kindness

Yep, we've all known the bosses who shout and are rude and belligerent, but, like the dinosaurs, they are a dying breed and we can move on. People are entitled to the following:

* Respect
* Civilized behavior
* Dignity

"WITHOUT THEM YOU ARE NOTHING; WITH THEM YOU ARE A TEAM."

If you can't give them these things, you shouldn't be a manager. But I'm sure you can. Creating a good atmosphere is easy. It comes from the top down. It is your job and your responsibility to be cheerful, considerate, polite, and helpful. Your people are one of your most important resources—your tools, your weapons of mass achievement. Without them you are nothing. With them you are a team. Use them kindly and don't abuse them. Be genuinely interested in them and their lives. If you don't have time—make time.

I guess the word I am looking for is "courtesy." An old-fashioned concept, I'll grant you, but one that gets mountains moved, doors opened, and staff working shifts they would normally have refused to do.

Inspire Loyalty and Team Spirit

"You can always find reasons to work. There will always be one more thing to do. But when people don't take time out, they stop being productive. They stop being happy, and that affects the morale of everyone around them."

Carisa Bianchi, chief strategy officer, TBWA/Chiat/Day

If you work together, chances are you are seeing more of your team than you are of your family. And your team is seeing more of you than of their families. If this is the case you had better all get along. Now you don't have to love each other, but you do have to be a family. And the best way to do that is to inspire loyalty and create a team spirit. You, as the manager, have to be the head of the family.

"CHANCES ARE YOU ARE
SEEING MORE OF YOUR
TEAM THAN YOU ARE OF
YOUR FAMILY."

You have to be respected, looked up to, trusted, and relied upon. Strong stuff. Can you do all that? Of course you can. All you have to do is this:

* Reward them.
* Praise them.
* Be kind to them.
* Trust them.
* Inspire them.
* Lead them.
* Motivate them.
* Grow them.
* Genuinely care about them.

These are the kinds of things that are easier to say than to do, and there's a temptation for you to skip down the list saying "Yes, yes, I do that." Now take a minute and go back and really think about each one. Do you *really* do that? Could you do it better? Are you absolutely sure you don't *think* you do it, but perhaps not actually do it? What people think they do and what they actually do can be very different indeed. Find somebody you can ask for honest feedback. Ideally one of your team—if not, somebody who sees you with your team. What do they say you do?

I once worked in competition with another company. A manager from the other company lived with one of my team members. She told John, my team member, all her boss's plans, figures, results, future promotions, etc., and I was able to beat him every time. Now why didn't she pass on all my stuff to her boss, seeing as she obviously discussed work with John? Simple. She didn't like her manager. And that was his fault entirely. He was rude to his staff, abusive, uncooperative, and unkind. Was I a soft touch? No way. I was strict and businesslike, but I treated my team with respect. I didn't have to do much because my competitor was doing enough wrong to make me look good.

Fight for Your Team

"It's a very difficult job and the only way through it is we all work together as a team. And that means you do everything I say."

Michael Caine in *The Italian Job*

At some point you'll have to fight for more resources, extra staff, more money, bigger and better offices, better facilities, more flexible hours, bigger doughnuts, whatever it takes to keep your team happy and content. And that means you have to be possessed with lots of self-confidence because you are going to have to go to your boss and ask—no, demand—that your team is the best, deserves the best, needs the best, will carry on giving of its best if it gets given the best, and you aren't going until they agree to provide the best.

And boy had you better be able to back this up. This means you have to have a great team delivering great results. You have to be one brilliant manager. And that's why most managers don't fight for their teams. Not because they don't think the team deserves it, but because they don't have the confidence in themselves to demand it. They are frightened they will have to justify it and they can't.

First build your team, then build your case, and then you can go and demand better and bigger. You have to be able to back up your demands—sorry, polite requests. Better still, have the financials to justify them.

If you don't get what you ask for, don't sulk—merely ask, "So what do I have to do to get this?" If they say, "Increase productivity by 10 percent," you've got them. All you have to do then is make those numbers and you've got what you wanted. To fight for your team means you have to get your team to fight for itself.

> "FIRST BUILD YOUR TEAM,
> THEN BUILD YOUR CASE,
> AND THEN YOU CAN GO
> AND DEMAND BETTER AND
> BIGGER."

Have and Show Trust in Your Staff

"It is happier to be sometimes cheated than not to trust."

Samuel Johnson

You have a computer I take it? Okay, it crashes from time to time—that's a given. You have a car. It breaks down for time to time, even if it's only a flat tire—that, too, is a given. Now you don't eye either of these warily, expecting them to let you down, watching them like a hawk in case they show any sign of breaking down, do you? No, of course not. So stop watching your staff like that. They are a tool to getting a job done. They will break down, crash, whatever, from time to time, but we accept their limitations—Rule 11—and we allow them to make mistakes—Rule 10—and we accept that we aren't managing them but instead their processes.

And if you can make that move to trusting your staff, you must show them that you are doing exactly that. Trust not only has to be done but it also has to be seen to be done. Sometimes you'll have to make a big show of really leaving them alone to get their jobs done.

You show them that you trust them by backing off, leaving them alone to do the job. Stop peering over their shoulders, checking every few moments, looking up nervously every time they move or cough or get up. Relax and let them do their jobs. You can still ask them to report back at the end of the day/week and encourage them to come to you to discuss any problems. Just make it clear

> ## "YOU SHOW THEM THAT YOU TRUST THEM BY BACKING OFF, LEAVING THEM ALONE TO DO THE JOB."

you trust them to do it, and you are always there if they need support or guidance.

But, I hear you say, what if I really don't trust them? What if I know they're a lazy, good-for-nothing, shiftless bunch of liberty takers? What if, indeed? Whose team is it? Who employed, trained, and kept such a bunch of monkeys?

Sorry, but sometimes we need to face the reality. If you can't trust your team, you need to look to your own management skills—or keep reading. A good team leader (that's you) has a good team following them. If the team is faulty, then the leadership has to be challenged—that's not going to be you. If the team is right, you can trust them. If the team really can't be trusted (and are you *sure* about that?), then it needs to be changed.

Respect Individual Differences

"We are dedicated to promoting a culture of respect, which values diversity and fosters an appreciation for the rights and individual differences of others."

Prince Edward School's beliefs

I have several children. I expect them to operate as a team. But I am also shrewd enough to realize they are all completely different and if I try to treat them all the same, apply the same rules—apart from the discipline ones—I'll get a mutiny, or chaos. Now one of them—and I'm not mentioning any names here but they will know which one I'm talking about—can't be hurried. Not ever, not anyhow. If you shove, he digs his heels in and can't be moved. He has to be lured, enticed, seduced into being quicker. But I have another son who constantly has to be slowed down. I have to respect—and work with—their individual differences. I simply have to.

Now your team is just the same. Some members can be hurried and others can't. Some will need to be slowed down and others you need to speed up. Some will come to work with a cheerful smile, others are best not approached first thing in the morning. Some will be terribly good with technology and others won't. Go back to what Belbin says in Rule 2 and see how everybody in a team has something different to offer—and that difference is what makes your team superb.

With my children if I need something done fast, I know who to call on. If I need a slower, more methodical approach, I select another child.

You don't have to let anyone get away with anything just because they are different—keep the discipline rules in place—it's more in the way you treat individual differences, the way you select tasks and the way you expect those tasks to be carried out. We are all different, thank God—a world populated by people like me, even I realize, would be ghastly—and those differences are what make a great team pull together effectively.

So if you're managing a sales team, say, and most of the members are well dressed and articulate (like you), but one prefers casual garb and is more chatty with his customers, don't mark his cards as "not a company man"—judge him on the results he gets. If he makes his targets and his customers love him, then *vive la différence*.

> "DIFFERENCES ARE WHAT MAKE A GOOD TEAM PULL TOGETHER EFFECTIVELY."

Listen to Ideas from Others

"When people talk, listen completely. Most people never listen."

Ernest Hemingway

If you think you know it all, chances are you will be too busy listening to yourself and how great you are to have time to listen to anyone else. But I know that's not you. Everyone, no matter how lowly their position or task, has something to offer you. Try talking to the receptionist, the parking attendant, the cafeteria staff, the cleaning staff, whoever and whatever. And, most important, listen to people on your team. They are the ones in the know who have to work with the resources and the products. They are the ones at the cutting edge and they may well have ideas, good ideas. You don't need to consult them over every little thing but the big things . . . well, yes. Talk to them. Get their feedback, their ideas, their creativity.

> "TALK TO THEM. GET THEIR FEEDBACK, THEIR IDEAS, THEIR CREATIVITY."

You obviously have to be careful to make sure that although you are listening to them it is you who still makes the final decision. You might listen, but that doesn't mean you are going to act on every one of their ideas. Nip in the bud the feeling that if they suggest, you have to carry out. Therein lies terrible trouble. Listen, assimilate, and then decide based on what you've heard, your own experience and ideas, and what is practical. It's no good you listening and then not using their information and them becoming terribly despondent— "What's the use of telling the boss my ideas? They're never used."

You have to listen without giving the idea that you will necessarily use their ideas, so then they won't be disappointed when you do something completely different. But you can make them think their ideas were incorporated into your overall strategy.

Virtually every team member I have ever known could tell their manager something useful about what they as a team or a company are getting wrong, or how something could be done better. If you're open to this, ask good questions, and listen without prejudice (or talking over them), you're immediately in a different class than most managers.

Adapt Your Style to Each Team Member

"You are unique; you have specific skills that address your organization's perceived needs and attracted its leaders to hire you. You also have a style of working with others that most likely has become an established pattern in your life. To the extent that your style of doing things fulfills the needs of the organization and its members, you will be successful."

Stephen C. Rafe, president, Rapport Communications

Adapting your style does not mean you have to be a chameleon. It means you have to be sensitive to your team's individuality and work with it. You may have outgoing members who like to be praised in public and then you might have quieter, more introspective members who would shrivel up and die if praised in public and prefer to be told they are doing a good job privately. There, you've changed your style without changing your skin, spots, or personality.

I have one team member, a very good one, who does her job superbly but who absolutely hates appraisals and would do anything to get out of them. She loathes having to talk about herself in any way—and this borders almost on a real phobia. I have to change my style with her considerably when carrying out a six-month appraisal because if she knows I'm even thinking about doing one she'll hyperventilate and have a panic attack.

> ## "YOU HAVE TO BE SENSITIVE TO YOUR TEAM'S INDIVIDUALITY AND WORK WITH IT."

And then I have another team member who greets me each morning with a very cheerful, "How am I doing, boss?" Now he really likes talking about himself and would happily be given a daily appraisal—if I were to let it happen. Both team members do their job extremely well—they wouldn't be there if they didn't—but they do need handling in a completely different way. I want them both to continue doing good work, and I have to handle them differently to get the best from them.

Similarly, some people like to be left alone, to create opportunities and make things happen, and they will come and tell you if they need help (the bright self-motivators), and others will need you to direct their actions more and give them specific projects to do. Don't overmanage the former—they'll resist and they'll get irritated (and quite possibly quit). Equally, don't undermanage the latter or they will feel stressed by a lack of structure to their job and won't work hard. Think about the individual. Think about what they need and what motivates them, and adapt your management style accordingly.

Let Them Think They Know More Than You (Even If They Don't)

"Of course I don't look busy, I did it right the first time."

Bumper sticker

This one is so simple, and yet I bet very few managers use it. And why not? It makes people feel really special and important. All you have to do is say to your staff, "You know about this, what do you think?" The key principles to this rule are as follows:

- Ask their opinion.
- Get their ideas and views.
- Give them more responsibility than they ever had before— you'll be surprised how people always rise to a challenge.
- Discuss important issues and news with them.
- Encourage feedback.
- Never dismiss them as being "mere workers."

Even if you *know* you know more about a subject than they do— still do it. They feel good. They perform better. They learn from your conversations. Maybe you learn too.

And while you're doing all this, take them through the entire process of your industry so that they don't get stuck in a rut of one department. You have to let them see their important role in the overall scheme of things, how their contribution is valuable and helpful and how the whole thing would flounder without them.

Treat them as you would a valuable client you were showing around. Let them in on your industry's secrets: "Well, we use the new XP8 coatings on our silicon chips, unlike Mathers and Crowley who still use the old XP5, but I expect you know that anyway, but do keep it under your hat because it's how we outsmarted them and got that huge contract with the DVLA last year."

Keep them informed about developments in your industry— perhaps you could subscribe to your industry's newsletters and magazines, technical journals and papers, that sort of thing—so that they think you are assuming they are interested, informed, know more than perhaps they do. This will encourage them to keep learning and wanting to know more.

> "ENCOURAGE THEM TO
> KEEP LEARNING AND
> WANTING TO KNOW
> MORE."

Don't Always Have to Have the Last Word

> "Everyone should be quick to listen, slow to speak and slow to become angry."
>
> James 1:19

Yes, yes, I know you are the boss, the manager—and a damn good one, may I say—but you don't always have to have the last word. This isn't like being kids in the playground.

If people on your team disagree with you openly, then there are two possible reasons why: Either they feel confident enough to engage in debate (in which case you ought to appreciate that) or they are out of line and you aren't imposing discipline enough to stop them. It may well be a warning sign that things are wrong or a sign that things are very right—only you can judge.

If they are out of line and there's a discipline issue, obviously you need to deal with that in private. Otherwise, remember that your staff are grown-ups. You have to give them room to be real people and that means they will sometimes disagree, argue, and get upset. That's fine in a good team where people can vent and nobody gets offended. It obviously doesn't work in a poor team.

It doesn't pay to always have the last word or always be right or always correct staff on every little thing. Sometimes, whether they are right or wrong, it's best to let it go. Know the difference between things important enough that you need to have the last word, and things where it really doesn't matter.

Understand the Roles of Others

"The problem is that we don't educate staff in the 'bigger picture.' In this case, that bigger picture relates to what other people do, their various expertise, and the relationship of other employee's jobs to each other."

Robert Bacal, *The Complete Idiot's Guide to Dealing with Difficult Employees*

I used to believe that to be a good manager I had to be able to do not only my own job—managing—but also everyone else's job as well. And probably, I thought in my heart of hearts, I should be able to do it as well as them if not better. Thus, I figured, if there was an emergency I could step into the situation and do their job and everything would carry on functioning. Yep, I bet you're there before me. If I were to step into their job, who would be doing mine?

Answer, of course: nobody.

The key is to have a practical understanding of what all the jobs entail but realize that you don't need to be able actually to do them. Yes, you do need backup in the event of a crisis, but it ain't you. You're better off right where you are—managing. To understand the role, the best way is to know what problems it solves and how it works. But you don't need to be able to do it as well as your team member does—that's why you pay them. Something about keeping dogs and barking yourself—you need to know

> ## "YOU DON'T NEED TO BE ABLE TO DO A ROLE AS WELL AS YOUR TEAM MEMBER DOES—THAT'S WHY YOU PAY THEM."

what job the guard dog does, but you don't need to go around biting burglars to fully appreciate it.

And often you'll employ someone for such a specialized job you wouldn't know where to begin. You might be the manager of a power plant, but you don't need to know how to calculate the shelf life of plutonium. But you do need to know that you employ someone who can do that job for you.

It's also important for your team to have an understanding of what everyone else does. This certainly helps create a team spirit and a sense of loyalty.

Ensure People Know Exactly What is Expected of Them

"It certainly sounds simple enough—just tell people what you want them to do so they can get on with the work. Unfortunately, all too often people are told to get on with it without knowing what is expected of them. They come out of large group announcements wondering what any of this has to do with them."

Chris Edgelow, Sundance Consulting

It's easy to give someone a job description and a contract and then sit back and expect them to complete the job. Trouble is, it leads to a lot of confused people and wasted time. Better to let them know right from the beginning what is expected of them.

> ## "LET THEM KNOW RIGHT FROM THE BEGINNING WHAT IS EXPECTED OF THEM."

RULE 30

And what is expected of them? Well, it's a whole lot more than just the job itself. You have to think through every individual role and what *exactly* is expected of that person.

It's vital that people know what part they play in any strategic plan and what is expected of them as a result. It's essential that team members know the values and standards of the team and the company, and what's expected of them in attitude and behavior (open? honest? imaginative? caring? can do?). It's also about them being clear on emotional requirements, punctuality, working overtime, behavior toward colleagues, crisis management—everything.

For new employees, this is helped if you have a "buddy" program where each new person is linked to someone more experienced who can show them the ropes.

Oh, and some guidelines on relationships at work. It's only fair that everyone knows what is expected of them in any given situation—you can't go telling off someone for hoarding paper-clips from the supply closet if it hasn't been spelled out to them that they can't do that sort of thing— "But we always did it at my previous place of work and no one complained."

Use Positive Reinforcement to Motivate

"So why should a manager change? Simply because results will get much better if he or she does it right. People will make conscious choices to contribute more of what they have to give in support of organizational objectives. What is there to not like about that?"

Larry Jones, *Driving Out the Fear*

If your staff does something good, tell them. And then tell them again. And again. Keep it up. Put it in writing. Send them a memo—something they can keep. Put it in the company newsletter. Add a note to their file. Whatever, but make it widely known they did good. This is a quick—and cheap (important, with your limited budget)—method of praising and motivating your team (and individual members, of course) and it lets everyone know you are monitoring, praising, and motivating.

When you praise people, make it simple. If they worked late to get a special order out, say, "Thank you for working late, we couldn't have done it without you. Your positive response to a difficult situation made everyone's job (especially mine) a lot easier. Thank you."* That's a whole lot easier than, "On the

---

* Reinforce by saying *thank you* again.

RULE 31

> ## "WHEN YOU PRAISE PEOPLE, MAKE IT SIMPLE."

evening of the 7th you were seconded to implement an extra shift duty, which you carried out in accordance with our wishes and for which we wish to convey our gratitude, blah, blah . . ."

Let them know why you are thanking them—*you made my job easier*—rather than just thanking them for what they did—*you came in for an extra shift*.

Be personal. Use "I" and "we", not "management." And say "thank you" in the same way as you would speak. "I want to thank you" is so much better than "The management wants to express its gratitude"—who speaks like that?

Praise as soon as the job was done, not a week later—do it the next day at the latest. And do it every time people do something beyond their normal brief. If they are asked to work an extra shift every week, that is just a part of their normal working pattern; instead, we are talking here of the extraordinary, the beyond the normal, going that extra mile sort of stuff.

If you reinforce positive behavior in this way, you will almost certainly guarantee it happening again. Fail to notice, to comment, to praise, and chances are your team will stop giving you their best—and who can blame them?

Don't Try Justifying Stupid Systems

> "Forcing a given team to adopt an approach that they don't believe in, either in their development process or in the language they're using to create the system, is a certain recipe for failure."

Luke Hohmann, *Beyond Software Architecture*

I was traveling on a train the other day (yes, there are still some of us who do) when we encountered a problem. It was fairly simple. Someone had messed with a security door at the dining car and triggered an alarm—or something. This brought the train to a standstill. But it did this in a very long tunnel. The train couldn't move until the fault had been rectified, which involved finding the train manager (they used to be called guards, remember?) and getting him to reset the triggered alarm. All fairly simple.

I was running very late for a meeting, so I asked if there wasn't a better system—i.e., letting the dining car staff reset the alarm. The train manager spent about 20 minutes justifying why this system was the best for everyone concerned, him, the staff, the train authorities, everyone that is except me—the poor passenger. It would have been much better if he'd just said, "Yes, it's a useless system and I shall recommend we change it, thank you for your concern."

And I bet you have a dozen useless systems within your organization—we all do. It's best not try to justify them. If you can't change them, put up with it, move on—but don't try hoodwinking the staff into thinking it's all just great. It isn't great, and you lose respect and trust if you try convincing people that it's fine when they know it's not.

I'm not saying you should go around lamenting loudly everything that is bad about your company—far from it, that road only leads to ruin. Remember, if you can't say something nice, don't say anything at all. Just don't try justifying something you know is stupid, especially to your team.

> "DON'T TRY
> HOODWINKING THE STAFF
> INTO THINKING IT'S ALL
> JUST GREAT."

Be Ready to Say Yes

"Silicon Valley has developed a 'genius' business model. You find a genius. You build a business around them."

Gordon Bell and Heidi Mason,

The Care and Feeding of "Intrapreneurs"

The good manager—that's you—tries to stay completely fresh. Not to get stuck in the same old ways of doing things. That means not having a default mechanism of "No, we don't do it like that." Instead replace it with "That's an interesting idea. How do you think that would work?"

What's more, you need to encourage people to come up with new ideas, as well as coming up with them yourself. Try ideas out. Take one new idea each week and give it a try. It might be fairly simple, "We'd like more choice of snacks in the break room, please," or something radical, "Listen up, guys, we're going to try a completely new approach to sales and distribution."

Obviously it makes sense to try out smaller ideas first to make sure your team can cope well with change, and then move on to the more radical ones later. Break 'em in slowly.

And as fast as you are introducing new ideas, get your team to do the same with their own individual jobs so that they don't grow stale either. If everyone has a new idea each week, that's a whole big bunch of new ideas by the end of the year for themselves and for the whole team. "I just thought I could speed the process up if I . . ." "Wow, I could take that idea and adapt it to my workstation and then I could . . ." "Yeah, and I bet they'd be really

> ## "IF EVERYONE HAS A NEW IDEA EACH WEEK, THAT'S A WHOLE BUNCH OF NEW IDEAS BY THE END OF THE YEAR."

interested in this in accounting because it could speed up the whole . . ." And so on.

Biggest challenge? Getting your team on board—everyone is resistant to change initially. If you hesitate, the whole team will also hesitate. If you maintain the passion, the whole team will be infected and become addicted to this. Believe me. Trust me. I know you already have enough to do, but we'll move on to delegating in a bit and that'll free up some time. Then you'll have more time to do this, which, in a way, is part of your real job—managing.

Encourage innovation. Reward good ideas. Create a culture where ideas are recognized (even if not adopted) and valued.

Train Them to Bring You Solutions, Not Problems

"Bring me solutions, not problems."

Margaret Thatcher, British Prime Minister (1979–90)

It's easy for staff to complain. I think it becomes a habit. You have to train your staff not just to complain. You can allow complaining but insist that if they bring you a problem they must also suggest a solution to the problem. Any idea that there is something wrong should always be met with, "And what would you like me to do about it?" If they resist, meet them with, "What do you think we should do?"

> "ANY IDEA THAT THERE IS SOMETHING WRONG SHOULD ALWAYS BE MET WITH, 'AND WHAT WOULD YOU LIKE ME TO DO ABOUT IT?'"

The best manager I ever worked for carried this even further and made us tell him the solution first—and then let him guess what he thought our "problem" was. It made it a game, which was sort of fun, but it also made us think on our feet a bit—made us be a bit lateral in our complaints. I was having a problem with security staff. I thought they were wiping the security camera footage without watching it, which was not good. This was my problem because if anything had happened I would have been blamed. I needed them to watch carefully but couldn't devise a solution to this problem—but I couldn't just go to the boss and complain that they weren't doing their job properly. I had to come up with a solution first.

Then it dawned on me that I didn't need to go to the boss. I could solve this one myself. I had to make sure the security staff thought there was something worth watching. I mentioned that some members of staff had been reported as having sex somewhere on the premises and it could have been covered by the security cameras, but no one was sure by which camera. There were cameras covering parking areas, offices, corridors, and storage areas in the basement. Result. The security guards started watching as if their lives depended on it. My boss was pleased because this was part of my job brief and he had noticed it wasn't being done properly and was going to chastize me about it. And I had come up with a solution to a problem without going to my boss and just complaining, "Oh, the security people aren't doing their job properly . . ."

Admittedly I had to come up with a fresh solution once the security staff realized they weren't going to see any smutty pictures—but it took them a long time, and they kept going back—just in case.

PART 2

MANAGING

YOURSELF

"The great danger is fossilization, becoming preoccupied with its internal tasks and systems and procedures, and losing touch with the world outside. And this will happen if everyone is concentrating on being efficient rather than being effective—in other words, if they don't follow *The Rules*."

Sir Antony Jay, creator of Sir Humphrey in *Yes Minister*
and founder of Video Arts, in his Forword to *The Rules of Work*

So those are the basic rules for managing a team. And obviously most managers have a team to manage. But all managers have themselves to manage as well—that's you. So the next set of rules is for you. These are rules to help you become more effective as well as more efficient. It's hard enough just getting through the day without trying to improve as well, believe me I know.

Being a manager is a tough job because it is always two jobs at once. You have to get your own work done and also be looking out for a team. The higher up the scale we go, the further away

> ## "IT'S HARD ENOUGH JUST GETTING THROUGH THE DAY WITHOUT TRYING TO IMPROVE AS WELL."

from our original job we get. And often no one bothers to train us as to what the new job—management—actually entails. Sure we go on the odd course—and some are very odd: I speak as one who has made Lego bridges, done jigsaws that are face down, been on canoeing weekends and all in the name of management training—but we don't specifically train to be managers. Management is something we sort of pick up as we go along. Sure there are a few good instinctive managers, but invariably we stumble along picking up the odd hint and clue here and there—it's a very hit-and-miss operation.

And a lot of what we are taught is fairly obvious. What I'm doing here is giving you the unwritten stuff—the stuff you don't get on those canoeing weekends.

Get It Done/Work Hard

> "Genius is 1 percent inspiration, and 99 percent perspiration."
>
> Thomas Edison

The fundamental rule of management, I'm afraid, is get the basic job done, get it done well, and work very hard at it. No good being a fantastic people manager if you let the basic job slip. You may have to get into the office earlier than anyone else, earlier than you've ever gotten there before, but get in early you must.

Once you have cleared your work out of the way you can concentrate on managing your team. Paperwork has to be done efficiently and on time. This isn't the place to go into lengthy training sessions on time management and the like, but basically you will have to be

* Organized
* Dedicated
* Ruthlessly efficient
* Focused

No choice I'm afraid. You have to knuckle down and do it. Management isn't hanging around issuing orders and looking cool. It's actually about what goes on in the background—the work being done where no one sees it.

And if you want to know if you are being a good manager now—take a look at your desk. Go on. Right now. What do you see? Clear space and order? Paper everywhere and piles of unsorted stuff? Do the same with your briefcase, files, computer even. Order or disorder?

> ## "YOU HAVE TO KNUCKLE
> ## DOWN AND DO IT."

You have to use whatever tools you have at hand to make sure the work is done, done well, and done on time. Make lists, use pop-up calendars on your computer, delegate, seek help, stay up late, get up early, get up earlier—obviously you still need to refer to Rule 71: Go Home, You Have to Have a Life. But get that work done and learn to be ruthlessly efficient.

Set an Example/ Standards

"Are you telling me that you built a time machine out of a DeLorean?"

"The way I see it, if you're going to build a time machine into a car, why not do it with some style?"

Michael J. Fox and Christopher Lloyd in Back to the Future

If you come in late, argue with your customers, are disrespectful and produce shoddy work, chances are your team is going to go to fall apart. If, on the other hand, and I assume this is more like the case, you arrive not only on time but early, do your work well and on time (*see* Rule 35), behave like a decent, honest, civilized human being and use your talent, chances are your staff will go to the top.

Everyone needs someone to look up to, someone they can respect and want to emulate. Sorry, friend, but that someone is you. Tough call I know. If you think heroes are so out of date, old-fashioned, and redundant, then think again. Every one of your team has a special relationship with you. You are their leader, their inspiration, their boss (there's a word to make you shudder, but that's what you are), their mentor, guide, teacher, hero, role model, champion, defender, guardian. To be all these things means you have to set an example. You have to play the part. You have to set standards. You have to be that role model.

> ## "YOU'VE GOT TO GIVE YOUR STAFF SOMETHING TO ASPIRE TO."

The bottom line is: If you don't care, why should they? You've got to set an example in everything you do. Think before you speak. Consider how you react. "Do as I say, not as I do" doesn't work. Be what you want to see in them.

You've also got to go beyond that and raise their stakes. If you're going to build a time machine, then do it with a DeLorean. You've got to give your staff something to aspire to, something to want to raise themselves up to. That's you.

Ideally, you'll have some style, some flair, some spark of originality that will set you apart from the herd—we're thinking Lauren Bacall and Cary Grant here, not Meatloaf and early Madonna.*

You've got to look the part, act the part, do the part—method acting here: Feel the manager, think the manager, be the manager.

---

* No offence, both make really good albums and are superb rock stars, but as role models for managers they don't make the grade.

RULE 37

Enjoy Yourself

> "The more I want to get something done, the less
> I call it work."
>
> Richard Bach

I'm going to be blunt now. If you're not enjoying what you do, then get the hell out and make room for someone who *is* going to enjoy it. Rule 38 may put things into context, but for the moment we need to get you feeling good about what you're doing. Enjoying work is about taking pleasure in a job well done, having an inner smile, finding something to laugh about and not taking it *too* seriously. (No, this does not mean you laugh *at* people or fail to do your job to the very highest standards.)

Enjoying work is about seeing your job, your role, in a much bigger context. You can be hardworking and you can enjoy yourself—you can do both. You can be productive, effective, efficient, industrious, sober, and reliable and responsible—and yet still be having fun. It's your choice. No one told you that you had to be serious and uptight. All you were hired to do was your job.

> "NO ONE TOLD YOU THAT
> YOU HAD TO BE SERIOUS
> AND UPTIGHT. ALL YOU
> WERE HIRED TO DO WAS
> YOUR JOB."

The best bit is that if you learn when to be serious and when to let up and find humor in a situation it will have a magical effect on those around you.

And if you work in a place where serious and uptight is the norm, here is a secret just for you: No one knows what is going on inside your head. No one. Just so long as the exterior is what they want, the inside can be whatever you want.

Don't Let It Get to You

"We have pictures of you so-called mooners. And just because the pictures aren't of your faces doesn't mean we can't identify you. At this very moment those pictures are on their way to Washington where the FBI has experts in this type of identification. If you turn yourselves in now, you may escape a federal charge."

Eve Arden in *Grease*

If it all gets too much, remember it's just a job. Sure, one we care about and try to do to the very best of our ability. One we worry about and think about when we're not at work. One we would like to make better and improve and be more effective at.

But it is only a job when all is said and done.

Look around you. You'll see the ones who think that what they do is central to the earth's movement or vital to the well-being of the entire planet. Nothing could be further from the truth. Enjoy it by all means. Take it seriously and give it all you've got, but remember it is just a job and it can be replaced, you can be replaced, the world will go on.

Not letting it get to you doesn't mean not caring or not taking pride and pleasure in what you do. No, it means putting things into context so you can go home and turn it off. Don't let it eat away at you or make you unhealthily stressed.

RULE 39

Know What You Are Supposed to Be Doing

"You'll excuse me, gentlemen. Your business is politics, mine is running a saloon."

Humphrey Bogart in *Casablanca*

So what are you supposed to be doing? It's very easy to think you know, but do you really? It's like when your boss says, "I want this done as soon as possible." Now that's really easy isn't it? Well, actually no. As soon as whose idea of possible? Your's? The boss's? And does "want" imply a wish or a need? And "done" is open to all sorts of interpretation. I know I'm being picky and pedantic, but I'm illustrating a point here. You know you have a team and you have to manage it. You know you have budgets and numbers and targets and they all have to be met. You know you have a forward-looking strategy and you would like to implement that. You know you have a contract and a job description.

But what are you supposed to be doing? What's your priority? What's the end point? What's the goal? Has anything changed recently. (Senior management sometimes have a way of changing their minds and expecting you to know telepathically.)

I once worked for a senior manager who, to all outward appearances, wanted my team to be successful and productive but who seemed to be hampering my every move. Whenever I wanted to make changes that would drastically improve our numbers, he hesitated and delayed and wouldn't make a decision. I couldn't figure out what I was supposed to be doing. I wanted to run the department for him as well as I could, but he seemed to be putting obstacles in my path. Eventually I discovered that another

> ## "WHAT'S YOUR PRIORITY?
> ## WHAT'S THE END POINT?
> ## WHAT'S THE GOAL?"

department—run by a relative of his—was supposed to be the winning team. I wasn't allowed to be the golden boy because that was the role for his young nephew. He wanted me to fail so young Sam could look good. I was supposed to be useless. Once I had that info—what I was supposed to be doing—I could work effectively with it. You've got to know what you're supposed to be doing.

Know What You Are Actually Doing

"You can't sail her with just two men. You'll never get out of the harbour!"

"Son, I'm Captain Jack Sparrow. Savvy?"

Johnny Depp in *Pirates of the Caribbean:*
The Curse of the Black Pearl

So what are you doing? Important but overlooked rule, this one. Go on, answer the question, what are you doing?

To answer this you need to have long- and short-term plans formulated. If you haven't got a plan, you don't have a map. If you don't have a map, you'll never find the treasure. If you know who you are and where you are going, you are indeed Captain Jack Sparrow—you're a pirate and clearly so.

> "IF YOU HAVEN'T GOT A PLAN, YOU DON'T HAVE A MAP. IF YOU DON'T HAVE A MAP, YOU'LL NEVER FIND THE TREASURE."

So, are you laying the groundwork for future promotion? Marking time until you decide what to do? Counting down the days until you retire? Collecting information so you can go to a rival and use it profitably? Waiting to be head-hunted? Learning more about the industry so you can make a sideways move? Enjoying yourself and having a ball? Doing a hatchet job for the management and laying off a third of the workforce?* Trying hard to be noticed by senior management? Working hard just to do a good job and stay ahead of the game? Building a social network to have fun with? Stealing ideas, resources, staff, and machinery to start your own rival business. (Oh, I've seen this done, and a very successful job they made of it too—they knew exactly what they were actually doing.)

There are no right and wrong answers. Well, actually a wrong answer would be, "I haven't a clue." You have to know what it is you are *actually* doing. Not what you are *supposed* to be doing. Not what you *want* to be doing. Not what the company *thinks* you are doing. But what you are *actually* doing. Once you know that you can work miracles because you have secret knowledge. Perhaps everyone else also knows; perhaps no one else knows. But *you* know and that is the important thing.

Now have a quick look round at your team and tell me what each and every one is actually doing. Good exercise.

---

* I knew a general manager of a big engineering concern who was brought in to do exactly that—and the workforce knew it. His first mass meeting was greeted with boos and catcalls. He stood his ground and just said, "I am not the enemy here. The enemy is the downturn in business. I am not the enemy, so don't shout at me." Worked like a charm.

Be Proactive, Not Reactive

"The greatest advancements of this century, the light bulb, the airplane, and the computer, were created by innovators—people who imagined things that did not exist and asked why. Being an outstanding employee requires a touch of this inventor's spirit, a determination to persistently strive to create value."

Bernie Milano, *How to be Proactive, Not Reactive*

I know, I know, it takes you all your time just to get the job done, the paperwork tidied and the plants watered without having to think about the future or be a whiz innovator. But the smart manager—that's you again—puts aside 30 minutes a week for forward planning. Try asking yourself simple questions: "How can I generate more sales?" "What can I do more expediently?" "How could I cut staff turnover?" "How can I convert more leads to sales?" "How could I streamline the accounting procedure?" "How could I move into another sector?" "How could I get my team to work harder, faster, brighter?" "How could I get them to brainstorm more freely?" "How could I hold meetings that wouldn't waste so much time?"

There is an old saying, "If you always do what you've always done, you'll always get what you've always got." And, by golly, it's true. If you aren't proactive you'll stagnate. And if you do that the crocodiles will bite your bottom. You have to keep paddling, keep moving forward in the water. Sharks have to keep moving forward

RULE 41

> ## "BE A SHARK. KEEP
> ## MOVING FORWARD."

all their life to keep water passing through or over their gills. They never stop. Be a shark. Keep moving forward. Because if you don't there will be plenty of others willing to do so.

And believe me, I know what it's like. You open your mailbox and there are loads of e-mails to deal with. Then there's the regular mail. Then there's the staff issues. Then there's lunch. Then there's the afternoon work to be done, and then there's a panic to get all the regular mail ready to go out, and then there's a quick cup of coffee, and then it's about time to pack it all in and go home, and there's this idiot telling me I've got to take 30 minutes out of a jam-packed day to think about the future. Yeah, in your dreams.

But that 30 minutes can be combined with another task. Once a week, I have lunch on my own and spend the time being proactive, thinking about the future, thinking of ways to be one jump ahead of the competition. But I do have to go out alone for that lunch or people come and interrupt my mental planning session.

Be Consistent

"I love the business casual look for the way it combines unattractive with unprofessional while diminishing neither."

Dilbert

If you were to wear a classy business suit every day and then suddenly, without warning, turn up in blue jeans and a worn T-shirt, chances are people would look at you askance.*

If you turn in good work and then one day hand in a pile of rubbish, people are going to think you've blown it.

If you treat the staff courteously until one day you blow your top and shout at everyone, they won't trust you anymore.

If you usually get in early and then one day stroll in around noon smelling of beer, they will stop taking you seriously and accuse you of being a drunk.

People need to know what to expect from you. You have to be consistent. You have to treat all staff the same. Do your work the same. You must avoid drawing the spotlight of gossip down on you. You must be blameless, above reproach (that's probably the same thing), honest, reliable, and dependable (again that's probably the same thing).

But you don't have to be dull or boring. You can be exciting, dynamic, stylish, adventurous, innovative, challenging—just make sure that whatever it is you decide to be, you stick at it and be consistently consistent.

---

* Try it, it's fun. If you don't know what *askance* is, look it up and then try it

Set Realistic Targets for Yourself—No, Really Realistic

"Your goals need to be realistic and achievable. If you set yourself unrealistic goals, you are only setting yourself up for the possibility of failure and disappointment. Larger tasks should be broken down into smaller, more manageable ones. This will make the large projects seem less daunting. It will also give you a sense of achievement on completion. When calculating how long you will need to complete a task, leave extra time in case the work takes longer than expected. This will relieve the time pressure."

Barbara Nance, *Returning to Learning, www.bbc.co.uk*

We're not talking budgets here or corporate targets. We're talking personal goals, personal objectives, personal bottom lines. You have to set them or you won't be able to determine whether or not you are a success. There's no point, by the way, of judging yourself against anyone else. I always wanted to be really good at sports but I can't run and fail miserably. It has always led me to believe I am a failure, but I found out the other day that there is a gene for good sporting skills and it is one I obviously don't have. Am I a failure? Nope, just genetically challenged, and I can't beat myself up about that. I am good at other things and I measure my success against

* How I was doing last year.
* How I was doing five years ago.
* How I'm doing against my personal targets.
* How I'm doing against my long-term plan.

There isn't another person in sight because measuring yourself against anyone else is a fool's game.

I once owned a motorcycle—a rather cool one and I loved it very much. I came alongside another motorcyclist at the traffic lights and looked his motorcycle over. "That's the one I want," I cried to myself in the splendid isolation of my helmet. He was looking at my motorcycle and obviously thinking the same thing. As the lights changed and we both roared away together, I realized he and I were riding identical motorcycles. Ah, the fickle mind, how it winds us up, beats us up, and plays tricks. Look at anyone and chances are there will be something to envy, but you don't know what goes on inside them. Walk a mile in someone else's shoes, they say, and chances are you'll be a mile away; but you've got their shoes, make a run for it.

So set yourself some targets but be realistic about them. I'm going to be Emperor of the World may sound impressive, but it is totally unrealistic (unless you're an American president perhaps?).

Make your targets challenging but attainable, realistic but a bit of a struggle—it's no good making them too easy, or too hard.

RULE 44

Have a Game Plan, but Keep It Secret

"Every job is a self-portrait of the person who does it. Autograph your work with excellence."

Anonymous

No one knows what goes on inside your head. No one knows what lofty heights you aspire to. No one knows what you're really up to—remember Rule 40: Know What You Are Actually Doing—so you can work on your game plan and be doing your job well at the same time. Your game plan should incorporate both long- and short-term goals—where you want to be, where you intend on being—and then you have something to match your success against—where you actually are.

Why keep it secret? Because the game plan of your corporation, your management team, and your boss may not exactly match your own game plan. This is a personal game plan and should be

> "YOUR GAME PLAN SHOULD INCORPORATE BOTH LONG- AND SHORT-TERM GOALS."

kept to yourself to protect your dreams and hopes and aspirations—there is nothing quite like having someone dampen your fireworks. An awful lot of management is having an external image—being able to look the part, to inspire confidence, to walk the walk. If people get wind of any game plan that deviates from that confident air of the perfect manager, they will lose confidence. You might be thinking of striking out on your own, but don't tell anyone or they will assume you are leaving any minute now, even if your plans don't allow for that for several years. If you have a game plan of rapid promotion, people will assume you are a high flyer and stop giving you long-term projects on the grounds that you'll be moving up too soon. And so on. Play your cards close to your chest and keep up the appearance of dedication, commitment, reliability, diligence, and stability— even if in your heart of hearts you are planning revolution, climbing Everest, or taking over the empire.

Get Rid of Superfluous Rules

"A self-reinforcing upward spiral: performance-stimulating, pride-stimulating performance."

Professor Rosabeth Moss Kanter, Harvard Business School

Ha, I can hear you thinking, "He's shot himself in the foot now. Get rid of superfluous rules, ha, in a book of rules?" Yep, get rid of superfluous rules. Not my rules of course, not your rules of course. Their rules, obviously. Let people on your team know that you are on their side and will streamline any procedures to enhance efficiency. That means old baggage has to go.

In any workplace there will be a mountain of red tape, bureaucracy, old rules left in place from previous management regimes—get rid of them all. Question everything you and your team do and make it work slicker and quicker by getting rid of anything that is redundant, unnecessary, or left over. This work is equivalent to clutter clearing—process feng shui if you like.

> "WHY DO WE DO THIS?
> WHY DO WE DO IT
> LIKE THIS?"

RULE 45

It's very easy to settle into a routine and to stop seeing things with a clear eye, a fresh vision. Every day you have to go into work and see it as an outside consultant would. Question "Why do we do this? Why do we do it like this?" I bet you'll find a lot of clutter and can eliminate it. I once worked for a company where every letter going out had to be vetted by a senior office secretary. She was a bit of a dragon to say the least, and if you ever got on the wrong side of her your letters went straight to the bottom of the pile—and stayed there. Why did letters have to be routed through her? Beats me, but I had to work unbelievably hard to get rid of that bit of Dickensian nonsense.

Streamline. Save time. Make your people happier and more trusted. Simple, really.

Learn from Your Mistakes

"A career setback can be like a romance gone bad. If you don't learn from your mistakes, you're doomed to repeat them, most likely in your next job. Many professionals are so eager to flee a bad job or fearful of being jobless, they jump from one job mismatch to the next, just like some people do in their personal relationships. If you've been knocked down but haven't looked at what caused your stumble, you're setting yourself up to fall again."

Bradley G. Richardson, To Move Ahead Again,

Learn from Career Setbacks

We all make mistakes—we wouldn't be the wonderfully creative, innovative managers we are if we didn't. But some managers gloss over any mistakes they make. They cover them, bury them, forget about them. You, as a brilliant manager, won't do that. You won't beat yourself up over them, nor sit in a pit of misery over them, but you will analyze what went wrong, discuss with colleagues why it went wrong, and make a plan to prevent it from going wrong again.

Our mistakes could be anything from a badly handled appraisal, a lost sale, a badly thought-out report, a poor use of time or resources, a failure to meet a deadline—when you start to write down how many failures there could be, the list is endless.

Once you have made your mistake, the important thing to do as well as all the aforementioned is to find out the right way to do it next time. Being a manager is an ongoing learning experience. You never stand still and you never think you know it all—you don't and can't. But you can have trusted people to ask and good reference books at hand to guide you—especially if they are short, sharp, snappy, and practical.*

Mistakes are brilliant because they not only teach us where we went wrong but also how to fix it. You are a better manager, more experienced, and have a wider spectrum to call on when you've made a few errors. We all make mistakes—admit them, learn from them, and move on.

> "BEING A MANAGER IS AN ONGOING LEARNING EXPERIENCE."

---

* See, for example, Ros Jay, *Fast Thinking Manager's Manual*, Prentice Hall, 2001.

RULE 47

Be Ready to Unlearn— What Works, Changes

"I simply wish to encourage you that, irrespective of what you have learned in the school, always be ready to unlearn and relearn. Don't give up dreaming. If we all dream about a better world, I can guarantee you we'll get there."

Professor Muhammad Yunus, University of the South, Tennessee

You know how it is, you're sailing along doing what you've always done and suddenly you're not making your goals, sales are dropping, staff turnover is going up, things are falling apart. But you're not doing anything you haven't done in the past. You had a winning formula and suddenly it doesn't work any more. What can you do? Well, for a start realize that what once worked might change. And it can change so rapidly you didn't realize it until it's too late. Be aware of this, be ready and prepared to adapt quickly. You have to stay abreast of the following:

* Latest innovations in your industry
* New technology
* New terminology
* New methodology
* Changes in sales, market trends, staff turnover figures, targets, and budgets

Don't get stuck in any ruts. Be ready to spin on a coin if you have to. Good management is about adapting to change rapidly and skillfully. If you don't, you go the way of the dinosaurs.

> ## "GOOD MANAGEMENT IS ABOUT ADAPTING TO CHANGE RAPIDLY AND SKILLFULLY."

The same goes for all sorts of things—style of management with staff, for instance. You might have a way with them that has worked for years and all of a sudden it doesn't. You could persevere, but you might lose staff rapidly. Better to be ready to unlearn your old ways and adopt new ones. It could be you have changed, unknowingly, unconsciously. If we get stuck in ways of doing things, sometimes we change them without recognizing that change. We have to be alert to those changes that creep in.

Cut the Crap—
Prioritize

"We wants it. We needs it. Must have the precious!"

Gollum (Andy Serkis) in *Lord of the Rings: The Two Towers*

Gollum knew the value of prioritizing. He knew what he wanted—to the exclusion of everything else. Now there's a dedicated creature for you.

I used to work for a manager who was fond of asking who we worked for. If we said ourselves, he shook his head. If we said him, he shook his head. If we said the directors, he shook his head. And on and on. The only answer, he said, was the shareholders. And the only reason we worked, he said, was for the profit. Everything else was padding. Fair enough. We do work for the shareholders—whoever they might be. It might be yourself if you are a one-person band. They might be the directors if it's a family owned firm and not trading on the stock market. They might be millions of little people who have all invested.

So cut the crap. There is only one reason for being in business, no matter what anyone says—profit. To make money. If you're making your targets, good. If you're not, clear your desk out. Simple. Now you have a neat yardstick to judge everything you do. Ask, "Does this contribute toward the profits I am making, or not?"If it does, keep right on doing it. If it doesn't, throw it out.

When all is said and done, that is what it's all about. No money, no business. No business, no job. No job, no mortgage, car, bread on the table, or vacations in Tuscany.

RULE 48

> ## "NO MONEY,
> ## NO BUSINESS.
> ## NO BUSINESS, NO JOB."

I bet if you sit down and look at everything you do, a lot of it will be padding. Time to prioritize. Cut the crap and dedicate yourself to one thing and one thing only—the bottom line. And that's what separates a really sharp manager like you from all the others. That clear focus, that vision, that dedication. Go Gollum, go.

Cultivate Those in the Know

"There's no point trying to hide from the fact that people know people and that possibly along the line they might well use those connections to 'further their career'."

Obi from Active Slaughter (anarcho punk band)

Always remember it's not who you know, but whom you know. And in business there are movers and shakers and there are worker ants. You need to know who the movers and shakers are—and cultivate them. Often senior management have PAs that act as guards—you don't get to talk to God, but you do get to be brushed off by God's right-hand PA. You have to get on the right side of the PA, and that means charm and politeness, tact and discretion, gamesmanship and ruthless cunning. I once worked for a boss who used a business consultant as his sort of unofficial PA—she shielded and protected him from having to talk to his

> "YOU NEED TO KNOW WHO THE MOVERS AND SHAKERS ARE—AND CULTIVATE THEM."

staff. Her last name was Burton and everyone called her Mrs Burton, except those in the boss's inner circle, who called her JB.

I started to call her JB also and the first few times she looked at me quite horrified—I was only a junior manager and not entitled to do so. But I got away with it. After a few weeks, the boss heard me call her JB and assumed I had been accepted into her inner circle of close friends and colleagues. He started to give me more responsibility, which meant she started to give me respect as I was obviously one of his favorites—and they bounced off each other, each believing me to be the other's accepted one and I got preferential treatment from both.

Networks of "people who know people" will never be dead because those in the know are the ones who still run that particular club. People in the know like to collect around them people they also know and therefore can trust. You have to get to know those around those who need to be known: Cultivate them, then become one of those around those in the know—and then become one of those in the know. What you do then is entirely up to you.

Know When to Shut the Door

"No other technique for the conduct of life attaches the individual so firmly to reality as laying emphasis on work; for their work at least gives them a secure place in the human community."

Sigmund Freud

Keeping an open-door policy as a manager is basically a good idea, but there comes a time when you have to know it is time to kick the door shut so that you can

* Get some work done.
* Have a meeting in private.
* Let your team know you don't want to be disturbed.
* Let the team know you really are the boss and not really one of them at all.

Obviously a good manager, such as yourself, likes to have an open-door policy so that the staff has access to you when and as they need. But there are times when it is necessary physically and psychologically to create a barrier. You see, the real secret of good management is that no matter how friendly you are with the team there comes a time when it is essential that you are actually the boss.

> ## "THERE ARE TIMES WHEN IT IS NECESSARY PHYSICALLY AND PSYCHOLOGICALLY TO CREATE A BARRIER."

Ruling by democracy is all very well; meetings and committees are fine; joint discussions are rewarding. But when push comes to shove, you have to be prepared to take charge and that means you have to fly by the seat of your pants, make the tough calls, and be the boss. And occasionally shutting the door reinforces that. You don't have to be a cruel or harsh or dictatorial boss, but a boss you must be.

If you are one of those managers who finds it hard to be assertive or "bossy," I suggest you practice shutting the door. It is a deeply symbolic gesture about who controls your environment—you. Do it a few times and the team will get the message. Once you've got used to it you can control who sits down in your office and how long they stay. It is essential for employees to take you seriously, for you to stamp your authority on the situation. Shutting the door symbolizes you are the manager—and this is a good thing, believe me. Oh, and it'll also mean you get some work done without interruption. Just don't do it too often—nothing is more frustrating than a boss who is never available.

Fill Your Time Productively and Profitably

"Dance like there's no one watching; sing like there's no one listening; love like you've never been hurt."

Professor William Purkey, University of North Carolina

"And work like you haven't got a boss—and don't need the money."

Richard Templar

Once you've learned to shut the door, you'll find yourself alone in an empty office. But to be the really great and effective manager you are, and are going to be, you don't coast or cruise. You get your head down and get the work done. And you get it done fast and effectively and efficiently. Then you do some work on your long-term goals, your game plan, and your business education (don't stand still—read something).

Working hard when you're not being encouraged with an electric cattle prod is a bit like working for yourself. You have to be motivated, dedicated, and focused. It takes practice and training. We all like to goof off. And that's fine every now and then. We all need thinking time—downtime. It is important, though, not to overdo it. Don't let the time bandits come in and steal a whole day.

RULE 51

"DON'T STAND STILL— READ SOMETHING."

Set little deadlines. Make short lists so you can cross off lots and feel good about what you've done. Get loads of fresh air, or you'll sleep too much. Don't drink alcohol at lunchtime, or you'll sleep in the afternoons. Go to bed early enough, or you'll be trying to catch up on sleep in the office.

Beware of time-wasting people. Practice telling people you've got something important and urgent to finish and can you come and see them later?

Beware of e-mails too—they have a way of sucking time. And they tend to make you terribly reactive— "Oh, I've got a clear in-box, all my work is done." But the truth is, work isn't replying to e-mails or composing e-mails—it is getting your sleeves rolled up and actually doing something; making phone calls, chasing people, creating sales, checking production, and filing reports. Get started, now. Be productive. Be profitable. Everything else can take a hike.

Have a Plan B and a Plan C

"I find it fascinating that most people plan their vacations with better care than they plan their lives. Perhaps that is because escape is easier than change."

John Rohn, the world's leading motivational speaker,

philosopher, and entrepreneur

You have to plan for disasters. You've got to build a "what if" clause into everything you do. If you don't, you'll be caught looking inept. Never assume it's all going fine—it isn't. Never assume you'll always do okay—you won't. Never assume technology will always work—it won't. Never assume you've got enough time—you haven't. Never assume they'll turn up on time—they won't. Never assume you won't forget things—you will. Never assume Plan A will work—it won't. Never assume Plan B will also work—one day that won't work either.

> "NEVER ASSUME YOU'VE
> GOT ENOUGH TIME—
> YOU HAVEN'T."

RULE 52

I think you might get the picture by now. When things go wrong—and they will—be ready to improvise, adapt, and overcome. Say you're giving a presentation and have mapped out the whole thing using PowerPoint, what will you do if there is a power cut? Technology failure? You must have worked out beforehand what to do when power fails or technology screws up or that order fails to come in—because they will. Maybe not today, but tomorrow lies waiting to catch you unaware, unguarded, unprepared.

Really good managers, of course, don't need Plan B or Plan C because they can think on their feet and are ready to cover their tracks at any time—ready to improvise. I think it wiser though to constantly ask, "How am I going to cope when this doesn't work?" Works for me every time.

Capitalize on Chance— Be Lucky, but Never Admit It

"I am a great believer in luck, and I find the harder I work the more I have of it."

Thomas Jefferson, U.S. President (1801–9)

If you keep your eyes open and your wits about you, there will be opportunities, chances, bits of random luck. If you are quick and clever and enterprising, you can catch the coattails of such moments and ride on the back of them. Such is luck. Grab it while you can, because it is a fleeting thing. You can't build it into a plan or a budget or a report, but it will happen all around you. In fact, the more you cherish it and nurture it and look for it, the more it will happen. We have to believe in luck or otherwise how could we attribute the success of people we don't like?

> "IF YOU WEREN'T SO GOOD AT YOUR JOB, THE LUCK WOULDN'T HAPPEN."

RULE 53

Now don't go building your career on luck, it doesn't work like that. I'm saying we all get a bit lucky from time to time, and when that happens you have to hang in there and go with it—and then keep quiet about it. You don't always have to tell the truth—and all that false modesty sucks. If you were lucky, say, "It was a lucky break," but say it in such a way that people know months of careful planning went into it, years of research, decades of experience—because that, frankly, is the truth. There is no such thing as luck, but there are moments of random opportunity based on all that work, experience, research, and planning. If you weren't so good at your job, the luck wouldn't happen. If you weren't such a good manager, you wouldn't be quick enough to seize those moments and utilize them.

Recognize When You're Stressed

"Opportunity is missed by most people because it comes dressed in overalls and looks like work."

Thomas Edison

The good manager stays well ahead of the stress game. And why? Because stress is counterproductive—it isn't profitable. The old image of the stressed executive popping pills, with high blood pressure but still pulling off fantastic deals is just that—old. The modern executive is laid back, unhurried, charming, thoughtful, careful, on top of their job. You don't need stress. You really, really don't. Yes, you need excitement, challenge, enthusiasm, exhilaration, and stimulation, but you do not need stress.

> "YES, YOU NEED EXCITEMENT, CHALLENGE, ENTHUSIASM, EXHILARATION, AND STIMULATION, BUT YOU DO NOT NEED STRESS."

Stress is just excitement and fun that has gone wrong. Instead of loving your job, you start to fear it. Instead of being excited, you experience fear. Instead of challenge, it's confrontation.

So how do you manifest stress? No really, how do *you* experience it? This is such a personal thing. I know when I'm under a lot of stress because I shout more, reason less, demand more, am polite less, rush more, am laid back less. But that's me. For you it might be smoking or drinking more or not sleeping or not eating (or eating too much or too hurriedly or too much junk food) or it might show as nervous exhaustion (sleeping too much), panic attacks, twitches, tics, irrational fears, inappropriate behavior, driving too fast (me again as well to that one). If you don't know what your signs are, ask somebody who knows you well—they will be able to tell you.

When I notice a couple of my stress symptoms I take time out to check

- Why am I stressed.
- What is causing the stress.
- What I can do about it.
- How I can stop it from recurring again.

I don't like being stressed (my children say I am a real pain) and there is no job worth doing that I'm going to allow to affect my health detrimentally. I know how to chill—I'm very good at lowering the stress levels once I notice they've crept up. I know what works for me. What works for you?

Manage Your Health

"The recommendation for a healthy heart may one day be exercise, eat right, and laugh a few times a day."

Michael Miller, MD, Center for Preventive Cardiology,
University of Maryland Medical Center

It's easy to put off managing your health. Do it now. The general advice is as follows:

- Eat properly—sitting down in a relaxed setting, taking time to enjoy your food
- Eat proper food—fresh, organic, lean meat, fresh fruit, salads, vegetables, roughage, no junk, no processed food
- Get a decent night's sleep—every night
- Stop worrying—laugh, have fun, enjoy something not work-related
- Carry out basic health checks regularly to catch major conditions in time, such as testicular or breast lumps
- Work in a comfortable and safe environment
- Get yourself screened from time to time for cholesterol levels, blood pressure, etc.
- Have supportive and loving relationships
- Have some sort of belief system to sustain you in times of crisis
- Exercise
- Watch your weight

- Drink moderately
- Don't smoke*

Of course you don't have to do any of this. You're a grown-up and can make your own decisions. But if you want to live long and prosper, it pays to think now.

> "IF YOU WANT TO LIVE LONG AND PROSPER, IT PAYS TO THINK NOW."

---

* Of all of them, this is the biggie apparently and will do more than all the others put together to contribute to your overall life expectancy and health.

Be Prepared for the Pain and Pleasure

"The biggest mistake we could ever make in our lives is to think we work for anybody but ourselves."

Brian Tracy, personal and business coach

Look, working for a living is always going to be a mixed bag. And the higher up you go, the more true this is. As a lowly accounts clerk, back when I first started out, I got used to being bored, idle, ticked off, frustrated, and sick of the job. By the time I had risen to being a general manager, I was strangely surprised to find myself also bored, idle, ticked off, frustrated, and sick of the job. But whereas when I was starting out I didn't expect any different, by the time I had risen to the heights I was totally unprepared for the same feelings. I guess I expected every day to be dramatic,

> "YOU HAVE TO ADJUST YOUR EXPECTATIONS SO THAT YOU DON'T GET TICKED OFF WHEN IT IS BORING."

exciting, utterly challenging, demanding, cutting-edge stuff. And when it wasn't, I was—I guess—disappointed.

Now, of course, I realize that not every day can be fantastic. Some days will be boring. Some days will be adrenaline-filled and dramatic—but not as many will be boring. You have to be prepared for the pain and the pleasure. You have to adjust your expectation so that you don't get ticked off when it is boring, and don't explode with pleasure when it is too exciting for words.

Trouble is, if it is boring, you might be tempted, as indeed I have been on many occasions, to liven it up a bit by being disruptive. It's best to sit on your hands and let the feeling pass. As a manager, you aren't allowed to be disruptive—except in an innovative way of course.

RULE 57

Face the Future

"The best thing about the future is that it only comes one day at a time."

Abraham Lincoln, U.S. President (1861–5)

Whatever you are doing now, things are going to change. It is inevitable that the future will soon be upon us. Things will change, they have to. People you now work with will leave your team. Your sales results will improve/slacken off. Your boss will retire/move on. Your customers will change. Your colleagues will be different. You, too, will change.

All these changes happen, and it is the smart manager who not only embraces them but is prepared for them. Earlier we looked at having a Plan B and a Plan C; well, this is different—this is not catering for a specific crisis but being fluid and flexible enough to stay ahead of the game. What this means is that when change occurs you can take it in stride and aren't thrown off course by it.

I once worked for a particular company that got taken over twice, in the space of a year. Each time the new people came in they had a whole series of changes to implement. They wanted things done "their way". This was fine, but after the first time we had barely gotten our breath back when the second takeover occurred. I watched a lot of people fall by the wayside because they couldn't cope with the stress of having to stay so flexible. I was nearly one of them myself. It was a hard time, but I saw then that resisting change was futile. Only by embracing the change could I survive—and not only survive but milk the situation to my advantage. The more I smiled and had a sort of "bring it on attitude," the more responsibility I was given for the change itself. Other managers played the oak in the storm, but I was the willow.

I bent and swayed and survived. They resisted, stood firm, and lost branches.

You have to face your own future as well. Will you move on? Have you grown bored with the job, the industry, your role in it? What turns you on today may not in 10 years' time.

> "RESISTING CHANGE WAS
> FUTILE. ONLY BY
> EMBRACING THE CHANGE
> COULD I SURVIVE."

RULE 58

Head Up, Not Head Down

"It's butt down head up, *not* head down butt up—you look like a bug that way."

Mark Maynard (aged 10), baseball player, Parker Bears

It's easy to adopt a head-down approach to life. It's harder to remain cheerful, head up. Is your glass half empty or half full? If it seems to be half empty, perhaps you need a vacation, a retraining schedule, a few new challenges, a new job, a new department, a new team—or simply a new approach. Life does tend to get fired at us at point-blank range and there is barely time to duck. The manager's lot is not always a happy or easy one and you get tired, despondent, bored, listless, and just about ready to quit. We all do from time to time. Being a manager can feel like a thankless task. You get stuff shovelled at you from all directions. I'm never sure whether it's better to be at the top shovelling stuff downward or at the bottom shovelling stuff upward, but I sure as hell know it's not great caught in the middle fending it off from above and below.

Head up is both an affirmation (repeat it to yourself constantly when encountering problems, but silently, only to yourself, or they will section you) and a physical instruction—you can physically and emotionally (and probably mentally) practice head up.

While looking in a mirror, keep your head up and say, "I feel really miserable." You will laugh. Try the opposite. Head down, and say, "I feel really happy." Again you will find it impossible and silly. You will laugh. But you have to be looking in a mirror. Perhaps you always look like that. Either way it is funny. You are funny.

> ## "PHYSICALLY AND EMOTIONALLY (AND PROBABLY MENTALLY) PRACTICE HEAD UP."

When entering a room, it is head up. When chairing a meeting, it is head up. When doing a presentation, it is head up. When greeting people it is head up. When talking to staff, it is head up. When talking to customers, it is head up. At the end of a long and busy day, when you go to bed, you can do head down—and go to sleep knowing you've been big and bright and bold all day. Well done.

See the Woods *and* the Trees

"Some people cannot see the wood, for the trees. I see the wood, and the trees and the small village beyond and what's more I have a flame-thrower."

Simon Munnery, stand-up comic, creator of the League Against Tedium

You've got to see the big picture. It's no good concentrating solely on what you do or what your department does. You can't even keep your gaze limited to what your organization does, or even what your industry does. You've got to see the wider view all the time. The good manager—that's you*—needs to have a good grasp of politics—both national and world—social history, world events, national intentions, international concerns, the environment, current legislation, proposed legislation,** and technological developments (ones that may or may not affect your industry).

But you've also got to keep a close watch on what is going on under your nose—your team, your department, your immediate surroundings, the fine details as well as the big picture.

---

* I keep saying, "That's you." You may wonder how I know. Because you are reading this. Bad managers think they know it all. You are prepared to read, to learn, to seek the advice of others, to widen your horizons, to have opinions, to stay abreast of current and new ideas and to keep an open mind by reading this far. That's good. You are good. Well done.

** No, not just legislation that affects your industry but all big proposed legislation. You'd be surprised how often the ruling will affect you.

The bright manager has to keep their eyes and ears open, their wits about them, their mind open to new ideas and innovations and trends. You've got to see the trees *and* the woods.

> ## "IT'S NO GOOD CONCENTRATING SOLELY ON WHAT YOU DO OR WHAT YOUR DEPARTMENT DOES."

Know When to Let Go

"You've got to let it go, let it go
You've got reason to be angry, but try not to let it grow;
When you brood on hate and bitterness till that is all you feel
You will never have the strength to stop the wheel."

"Let It Go" lyrics by Catherine Faber

Sometimes it's really hard to let go—to know when to stop. But some projects just aren't going to work. Some team members are never going to fit in. Some bosses are never going to be possible to work with. Some situations must simply cease. The good manager knows instinctively when to back off, to bail out, to retreat, to walk away whistling—pride intact and dignity in place. This rule is for you but also for all the people who get caught, fool around, and try to defend the indefensible. Come on guys, know when to quit, know when the dog is dead.

> "KNOW WHEN TO QUIT,
> KNOW WHEN THE DOG IS
> DEAD."

RULE 60

A good manager knows when to hold their hands up, "Yep, I messed up. It was my fault. I surrender." Invariably you'll be forgiven because such an honest, direct approach throws 'em off the trail and they don't know how to handle you.

If you don't know when to let go, you'll build up anger, resentment, stress, jealousy, pain. Learn to shrug and walk. You don't have to forgive or forget or anything, except drop it and walk away.

There is a myth in business that to get even is better than getting mad. But getting even is getting mad, it just takes a bit longer. Let it go. Concentrate on the next big exciting thing you can do.

Be Decisive, Even If It Means Being Wrong Sometimes

"I don't know what kind of people you're used to dealing with. Nobody tells me what to do in my place."

Karen Allen in *Raiders of the Lost Ark*

I bet you hate the type of manager who refuses to make a decent decision in case they make the wrong one—the prevaricating, indecisive, frightened manager who won't decide until it's too late or they get the decision made for them. I've worked for a few and there is nothing more irritating than someone who fence-sits because they don't know which way to jump—and all in the name of fear. They are frightened to decide in case they make a mistake—one that might cost them their job. Big deal. Better to jump and make a mistake than to sit there too frightened to make a move. Bring it on.

And suppose it does turn out to be the wrong decision. Well, sometimes out of big mistakes something bright and shiny and magical appears and we land on our feet and manage to look good despite sometimes not knowing what we were doing. This is the magical manager that I want you to be. The instinctive manager around whom anything can happen—and will. If you want to sit on a fence, go find another book to read.

Now I'm not saying here that you should make rash, ill-thought-through decisions. I'm assuming as a good manager that if it's that

> ## "BETTER TO JUMP AND MAKE A MISTAKE THAN TO SIT THERE TOO FRIGHTENED TO MAKE A MOVE."

kind of decision, you have looked at the evidence before you and weighed it, and maybe asked for views from others. It's that point in the process I'm talking about—the point where you are tempted to shirk the decision in case it turns out to be the wrong one.

This is about courage. The courage to be wrong sometimes. The courage to take a risk. The courage to be scared in a good way. (Sitting on a fence because you are scared is a lot different from taking a big decision and being scared but exhilarated.)

All you've got to do is look at the facts, weigh them, ask for advice, listen to your intuition, and then do it—make the decision. Be dynamic, be bold.

Adopt Minimalism as a Management Style

"Seek honest, minimalist management. Look for companies run by a team that explains things clearly and briefly. I'll admit, judging management honesty isn't always so simple. It's not as if the crooks out there come with black masks, striped jump-suits, and carry sacks with dollar signs on them. But you can tell a lot about the firm by reading an annual report or two, readily available. If management can't explain the business in plain English, move on to another firm. If you see phrases like 'creating knowledge-based values in emerging markets' . . . someone is trying to pull the wool over your eyes, you lazy Fool. Run."

Seth Jayson, "Stocks for the Lazy Investor,"
The Motley Fool, www.fool.com

Minimalism means not issuing lengthy reports. It means not issuing memos every 20 minutes. It means keeping rules to a minimum* and letting people get on with their jobs. It means mission statements that make sense, are clear and easy to understand, and are simple. It means management where managers use professionals and let them get on with their tasks in peace and quiet. It means managers who are secure in themselves and don't need to score points, bully, or interfere. Minimalist management is all about getting more by doing less. Yes, sure you have to be the boss, but it's more like steering a big ship—the tiniest touch of the wheel is enough. You swing that wheel violently from side to side and you're off course in an instant.

There is an old Chinese saying: "Govern a country the same way you cook small fish," i.e., don't keep fiddling with them or they fall apart. Manage a department, team, or company in pretty much the same way—gently, discreetly, and unobtrusively. Better to be understated than too obvious.

> "MINIMALIST MANAGEMENT IS ALL ABOUT GETTING MORE BY DOING LESS."

---

* No, not these rules, I mean the petty ones—you have to wear a tie, you have to have one doughnut, not two at coffee time, you have to address senior management as Mr/Mrs X and not use their first names, you have to park tidily, you have to wear sensible shoes, you have to . . . you know what I mean.

Visualize Your Blue Plaque

"The first official London plaques were erected in 1867 by the Royal Society of Arts at the instigation of William Ewart MP . . . In total there are about 700 official plaques and most of them are blue with white lettering."

www.blueplaque.com

When you write your bestseller and then die, you will get a blue plaque on the building where you were born, or lived, or wrote the damn thing—just so long as it was in London.* When I say "you" I don't mean you, I mean whoever it is that lives there after you've snuffed it. This blue plaque is there to commemorate the fact that you did a good thing while you were alive. If you didn't do your good thing—i.e., write your bestseller, add to the sum of human literacy, manage to afford to live in London—you don't get a blue plaque.

Now imagine that there is a blue plaque for management style and it's not limited to London. What would you get yours for? Would you in fact get one? Basically, how would you like to be remembered? I worked for a boss once whose style of management was quaint to say the least. As he came in each day, he would blast the first person he saw, and give them a complete earful about whatever they happened to be doing. Then he would go to his

---

* I'm fairly certain you have to be dead, but you don't have to have written anything. Being a musician is good enough—even Jimmy Hendrix got one.

> ## "HOW WOULD YOU LIKE
> ## TO BE REMEMBERED?"

office and have a coffee for half an hour. Then he would walk through the plant and compliment the first person he saw, tell them what a great job they were doing no matter what it was they were doing. I asked him about this and he said, "Keeps them on their toes. They never know where they are with me. I get more out of them if they are frightened." No blue plaque for you, Billy boy.

I've told this before because it still, after over 20 years, fascinates me as the worst, incompetent, bullying, stupidity I have ever come across. And he is still in a job—still employed by the same firm. Yes, he has hardly risen up the ranks, because he is still doing pretty much what he was then, back when I knew him, but he is still employed. I don't buy stock in that particular company—never have, never will.

I want a blue plaque. I want it for being the best damn manager there ever was. I want it for being good for my team, getting results, setting standards; for being a huge success and somebody they liked working for.

Have Principles and Stick to Them

"Dear . . . I have given your proposition a lot of thought. My main concern is that you want the items to be prepurchased for the XX Show. I feel this is not acceptable and is misleading the 8 million viewers who will be watching the show, as you have informed me. I have been in the antiques business for 30 years, and I feel my reputation would be undermined if an item that was prepurchased was placed in my antiques center and supposedly purchased there, and then went to an auction house to be sold at a loss. Because of this, I must decline your offer to use my premises as a backdrop for your show. In the short brief time I met you, you came over as a very nice person and I hope you are successful with the show. Yours faithfully . . ..

Genuine letter from an antiques expert turning down a very

kind—and obviously lucrative—offer from a television company

When you think about it, you've got to have principles. If you don't, you end up despising yourself or in debt or prison. You might end up like this anyway, but at least you could say, "But I have my principles." There has to be a line beyond which you will

> "THERE HAS TO BE A LINE BEYOND WHICH YOU WILL NOT GO. YOU HAVE TO KNOW WHERE THAT LINE IS DRAWN."

not go. You have to know where that line is drawn. No one else has to know until they ask you to cross it and then you can tell them. That line has to be a ten-mile-high solid steel wall. You can't go beyond it, no matter what.

So where would you draw your line? I've been asked to do things I didn't like. I've been asked to do things I found unpleasant. I've been asked to do things I found extremely irksome, but whenever I've been asked to cross my own personal line—which thankfully in a long business career has been only once or twice—I was able to say, "No," and stick to it. And each time I got a pat on the back rather than a trip to the unemployment office.

Follow Your Intuition/ Gut Instinct

"Sometimes you just have to follow your intuition."

Bill Gates, founder of Microsoft

If it is good enough for Bill Gates, I guess it ought to be good enough for the rest of us. Deep down inside you know when you're right, and you know when you're wrong. Sure we can cut off that inner voice, but if we do lose touch, then we really are in trouble. That inner intuition may not speak loud and clear all the time, but when it does you'd be crazy not to follow it. Trouble is your mind also speaks loud and clear—all the time—and we mix the two up and follow what we think is intuition when in fact it is fear or jealousy or another emotion.

So how do you tell? If when you're talking to somebody about a new system you are about to implement and, though they look positive, you feel an odd or cold feeling inside, pay attention to it. Take time to think why. Tell somebody else about it and see if it happens again. Go back to the plan and look at it from all viewpoints, considering all the stakeholders. Are you still convinced? Never be too proud or too lazy to get more feedback, to find a sounding board or to rethink a proposal or a decision if you've got a bad feeling about it.

Look at previous good or bad decisions you've made. How did you feel about them at the time? Did you, deep down, know a bad course of action was flawed before you followed it? Would you know that feeling again?

> ## "NEVER BE TOO PROUD OR TOO LAZY TO GET MORE FEEDBACK."

Developing your intuition is a hard thing to teach, but if you make a habit of "listening" to how you feel about something, your radar will improve and you'll begin to know when a gut feeling is telling you that something isn't right.

Be Creative

"Almost everyone is born with the capacity to be creative, but few realize it and such skills are often neglected or untapped. Lateral thinking is all about thinking "outside the box," breaking out of familiar thought patterns and coming up with new possibilities. It is one of the keys to improving creativity."

Lloyd King, lateral thinking expert,
author of the best-selling *Puzzles for the High IQ*

The good manager keeps a store cupboard full of creative techniques so that when they get stuck, when the team gets stuck—and you and they will from time to time—you have something to fall back on.

Being creative is about finding new and different ways to solve problems. You get stuck and start worrying and then you go off and tend your garden, do the dishes, fly a kite or whatever, and you get immersed in what you are doing and the answers bubble up to the surface.

Most creative techniques get you to switch off your conscious, thinking brain and start to use a deeper more intuitive part of your mind. And that part has a whole load of answers that we can't normally access. This is the part we can access during sleep or meditation or by using creative thinking techniques.

Watch what other managers do—the ones you admire and respect. They probably have a store cupboard of creative tricks. Borrow a few. Read up on creative-thinking techniques. Find out

> ## "GET IMMERSED IN WHAT YOU ARE DOING AND ANSWERS BUBBLE UP TO THE SURFACE."

what the bright managers are doing, thinking, trying out. Ask somebody not in your field what they would do. Don't be afraid to be wacky or off the wall—after all some of the best ideas have come from dreams.

Don't Stagnate

"A manager's job is to create stability and deal with reality. A leader's job is to stir emotion and set audacious, grandiose goals that shake the status quo. Too much management and you stagnate. Too much leadership and you get nowhere. Embrace the challenge of striking the balance. Do it well, and the results will surpass your wildest dreams."

The Management and Leadership Network

So are you a leader or a manager? Not really a fair question when we've spent the whole book so far making sure you are an effective, efficient, and startlingly good manager. But the really good managers are also leaders—they inspire and motivate, encourage, and enthuse. They draw people to them like moths to a flame. They are charismatic and dynamic and stylish. They are leaders indeed. But they are also good managers. Too much management and you stagnate. You have to revel in change, seek new challenges, stay on your toes, find new ways of doing things, motivate your team in new and exciting ways, introduce new technology and ideas, start trends, jump fences, and light fires. You can't be seen to stand still or moss will grow over you and you become a fixture and people stop noticing you.

I know it's difficult sometimes to see beyond today's work load, tomorrow's meetings, next week's directors' report. But you have to be moving or you will stagnate. Set aside a little time each day or week—only half an hour perhaps—to think up new ways of being revolutionary. Why? Because if you don't do this you

> ## "THE REALLY GOOD MANAGERS ARE ALSO LEADERS—THEY INSPIRE AND MOTIVATE, ENCOURAGE, AND ENTHUSE."

become bogged down in the day to day, the humdrum, the routine. Yes, you are a manager, but you are also an innovator, motivator, inspirer, leader, and trendsetter.

If the moss has already grown over you and people have come to regard you as part of the furniture, you will have to work very hard to shake off that image. Don't scare them with radical change—do it bit by bit.

Be Flexible and Ready to Move On

"Don't be irreplaceable. If you can't be replaced, you can't be promoted."

Anonymous

There will come a time when it's time to move on. Other jobs are waiting to be done. Other teams are waiting to be led. You may have to pack up camp and hit the trail. "Hell is in hello, heaven is in goodbye forever, it's time for me to go," sort of stuff.* Keep your eyes open for opportunities. Remember your long-term plan—and I bet it didn't include stuff like, "Stay here until I retire and/or turn to dust"—and keep looking to distant horizons.

Being a good manager, a fantastic manager, often means you get sought out, head-hunted, and poached. Be ready to be enticed away. Doesn't mean you have to go, but be open to offers—how flattering.

Stay on your toes and be ready to move sideways; be prepared to look at unusual opportunities. Be ready perhaps to go it alone if that's in your long-term plan.

Should you feel guilty at abandoning your team? No. You have a career and that involves moving on. Your team may benefit from a breath of fresh air coming in after you to blow the cobwebs away. I've left managerial jobs where the staff seemed genuinely surprised that I would dare to leave, to spread my wings and go

---

* Lee Marvin in *Paint Your Wagon*.

> ## "BE PREPARED TO LOOK AT
> ## UNUSUAL
> ## OPPORTUNITIES."

"elsewhere," as if it was a dark and dangerous country that would gobble me up. Of course, once I left I gained a reputation as a "deserter" for leaving, but better that than "good riddance."

Remember the Object of the Exercise

"Happy, fulfilled, stretched but supported people generally achieve the most at work and get the most from life. They drain a lot of swamps—and have a pretty good time doing it (strange though it may seem swamp drainage is a Very Enjoyable Occupation). However, many of us face a few alligators . . . those subversive obstacles that get in the way of a productive, high achieving but low-stress kind of life. Some of them we make ourselves, some of them are placed there by other people. Some of them just are."

Get Ahead; Give a Damn*

And the object of the exercise, my friend, is what? We all have a different agenda. You may say, "To make profits for the share-holders" (Rule 48), but you're just trying to gain favor by giving an answer you think I want. I don't.

Remember that even when you are up to your arse in alligators, the object of the exercise was to drain the swamp. There are many

---

* *Get Ahead; Give a Damn* is a little book of big ideas about how to be more suc-cessful and happier at work. Every penny of the cover price goes to help homeless unemployed people get back on their feet. You can get a copy from *www.pearson-books.com* if you are interested.

objectives, many swamp-draining exercises. You might see it as the next project, setting the next budget, getting through the next interview, week, or disciplinary interview. It might be long-term stuff, career in general, etc. And the alligators who bite your bottom could be colleagues, customers, clients, bosses, staff, family—you name it/them. But they do get in the way of draining the swamp.

This is a Rule about focusing so you don't get side-tracked by all the nonsense that goes on around you. Stay focused and keep the objective in your sights at all times—whatever it may be.

> "STAY FOCUSED AND KEEP
> THE OBJECT IN YOUR
> SIGHTS AT ALL TIMES—
> WHATEVER IT MAY BE."

RULE 70

Remember That None of Us Has to be Here

"There is no formula for success, but there is formula for failure and that is trying to please everybody."

Man Ray, painter, photographer, sculptor, illustrator, filmmaker, inventor, philosopher

I once worked with a fabulous manager. Sadly he is no longer with us, but I remember all the managerial stuff he taught me. He was one of us—seemingly. On the surface he played the company game, discreet, charming, efficient, hard-working, but deep down this man worked for no one but himself. Bob was a individualist, a rule breaker (but not these Rules—most of these came from him), nonconformist, maverick. He trod a fine line. He was Mr Cool Dude. Mr Management Should Never Be Seen to Be Done.

Sure he got the job done and done extremely well, but he was a managerial rebel. He and I were scheduled once to go on a manager's training course. Guess who failed to show up? Yep, Bob. He wasn't going to make Lego models for anyone.

I went. I made Lego models. I toed the company line. Guess who got promoted? Yep, right again. Bob.

So how did we get here? Ah, moaning. I moaned. Bob would say, "None of us has to be here." And he meant it. Literally. Literally none of us has to be here. We don't have to do the job. We can walk any time we want. This means we are here by choice. We have chosen to be here. We choose to be here each and every day.

> # "STOP MOANING—ENJOY IT OR LEAVE."

It is our choice. If we have chosen to be here then surely it means we are enjoying it—or we wouldn't be here? Right? If we aren't enjoying it, then we should choose not to be here.

Basically what Bob was saying to me was, "Stop moaning—enjoy it or leave." This doesn't mean you can't point out the things that are wrong, but if they aren't going to get solved you'd better learn to live with them. Enjoy it or move over and let someone else do the job who will. None of us has to be here.

Go Home

> "Many managers follow the notion of busy fools and confuse hard work with long hours. They think because they work 15-hour days and forget their children's names, they must be bloody good managers. The best sales manager I worked with never once worked beyond 5:30 p.m."
>
> Caspian Woods, *From Acorns—How to Build Your Brilliant Business from Scratch*

Another manager I worked with stayed late, got in early, skipped lunch, and kept his head down and worked hard every second he was there. Guess who got promoted over him? Yep, Bob again from Rule 70. Mr Cool Dude.

One of Bob's favorite lines, to me anyway, was, "Go home, Rich, go home. You've got a young family, go home and see them before they forget what you look like. Either that or send them a photo before they really forget." Naturally I went home. As did Bob, a lot. In fact, he was at work so little he got promoted again. His secret? His team, of which I was one, would have done anything for him. We went that extra mile. We would never have willingly let him down. Bob inspired loyalty in his staff in a way I've rarely seen since. He made all of us feel grown-up, trusted, treated in a respectful way. He never shouted, abused, demanded, overworked, or humiliated his team. I never saw him have to discipline anyone, ever. He was charismatic and charming, cool and relaxed. He cooked us all like small fish.

He said his secret was his family. For them he worked. He adored his children and would rather have been home with them than working. His love for them showed and he wore the badge of happy family man with great pride. He talked a lot about his kids and his wife and was obviously very happy with them.

He never stayed late because that would have been disloyal to his number-one priority—his family. This gave him great depth. He was well rounded and balanced. He was at ease with himself. He had nothing to prove at work because he was content at home. I've worked with some complete jerks and I can say the only thing they all had in common was a bad home life. Their base camp was corrupt and it showed. So, my dear friend, go home.

> "HE HAD NOTHING TO PROVE AT WORK BECAUSE HE WAS CONTENT AT HOME."

RULE 72

Keep Learning— Especially from the Opposition

> "The illiterate of the twenty-first century will not be those who cannot read and write, but those who cannot learn, unlearn, and relearn."
>
> Alvin Toffler, *The Third Wave*

We've all heard the manager who gets angry when the competition overtakes them. Or who complains about how unfair it was that they lost such and such an order. Or when a client leaves them, screams that they've been betrayed. Wrong, wrong, wrong. Believe me, if the competition is stealing your ideas, your customers, your contracts, your clients, your sales, your staff, and your income, then you have a) no one to blame but yourself, and b) been given a great opportunity to learn how to do it better.

Nothing teaches us better than a better competitor. What is it they are doing? What can we learn from this? How can we emulate them? How can we take what they are doing and really run with it? How can we grow our market share by outdoing what they are doing?

Spend some time each week checking what the competition is doing, because if they are effective (and competition invariable is) they will be checking out what you are doing. Spend some time getting to know—and sharing with—the competition. Look, if you have five main competitors and you share with them, you are giving each one a part of what you are doing. But the idea spreads and *five* will give you ideas, information, research, etc. We should never fear competition. Embrace it. It grows the market. It keeps you on your toes. It gives you a real learning opportunity—real as in it is actually happening and isn't a training exercise. And it doesn't involve Legos.

If you fear competition, what you really fear is your own incompetence. If you know you're doing a good job, the competition can't touch you. If you're not doing a good job, the competition can walk all over you—and you know it, just as you know you're not doing a good job.

> "IF YOU FEAR
> COMPETITION, WHAT YOU
> REALLY FEAR IS YOUR
> OWN INCOMPETENCE."

Be Passionate and Bold

"I love the moody, almost frantic style of Ramsey, always searching for the next great eating experience, passionate about his art."

Reader's review of Gordon Ramsey's *A Chef for All Seasons*

If you're not going to be passionate about your work, what are you going to be passionate about? Look, you spend more time at work doing work, living, breathing, and being work, than anything else except perhaps sleeping. You must be passionate about what you do. You're passionate about sex, but that doesn't last as long as your career. You're passionate about food, and you only eat three times a day—work is continual. You're passionate about your life, your hobbies, your family, your vacations. And yet an awful lot of people see their work as something to dread, a chore to be got through. If it's like that for you, then go home—and stay there. Make room for someone who is going to be passionate about it. But I'm positive that isn't you.

When I first started my career—of which I have had several—I read up on the industry before I started training. I read about its history, the famous people in it, stories about it, how it evolved and the legislation surrounding it, how certain traditions associated with it came about. I went into that job a walking encyclopedia of facts and information, anecdotes and history. And I had my breath taken away by how little everyone else in that industry knew. I was passionate, and it seemed no one else was. I found only a terribly small group of people who cared about what they did. Over the years I have met many others, but never enough.

RULE 73

> "ONCE YOU ARE PASSIONATE, YOU CAN BE BOLD, BECAUSE YOU HAVE THAT DRIVE, THAT ENTHUSIASM, THAT COURAGE, THAT EXCITEMENT."

Once you are passionate, you can be bold, because you have that drive, that enthusiasm, that courage, and that excitement. Being bold means you can take risks. And taking risks means they pay off—not all the time but often enough that you get a name for yourself as a high-flyer, a go-getter, a success.

Being passionate means caring about what you do. Not just going through the motions but really caring. Being driven—being constantly excited and enthusiastic. What you do makes a difference—it's not just about the money or the status or the perks. It's about making a real contribution to people's lives and the environment and society. If you're not passionate, what are you? If you are passionate, what are you passionate about? If not now, when?

Plan for the Worst, but Hope for the Best

> "If you decide to go out to these wild places and put yourself in these conditions, be responsible for yourself and those in your party. There are many requirements; good judgement, common sense, experience, and leadership are just a few. Unexpected things can and do happen . . . Be Prepared. Expect the unexpected. Always carry a bivvy sack on every climb. Be prepared to spend the night up there! Plan for the worst, but hope for the best!"
>
> Tim Driskell, climber

I don't expect you to carry a bivvy sack [space blanket] at all times, but I do expect you to prepare for the worst and hope for the best. What's your worst-case scenario? All the staff phone in sick because it's the World Series? You lose that big order? Sales slump to zero? Building burns down? Union strikes? Flu epidemic? Terrorist attack? Oil spillage? Health department close you down? All or any of these things can play havoc with your budget.

So what contingency plans do you have in place in case this worst-case scenario actually happens? Huh? Yep, thought so. You've got to have emergency plans, panic routes mapped out, procedures for crisis management, actions wrapped up and in the bag, replacement crews sorted, alternative sources of income laid down. You have to have a plan.

Now chances are you won't ever have to implement this plan. With luck and divine intervention it will always remain a plan— nothing more. But a plan you have to have.

Now, you are allowed to hope. Hope it ain't never gonna happen. Hope the sun will forever shine. I was once asked by a special committee what I would do in the event of a major bomb scare at the company where I worked. My answer, "Hope it's a hoax," made them laugh but earned me no brownie points at all. "What about a plan?" I was asked. "Oh, I've got one of those as well," I said and I may have recovered about half a point. Have a plan— and a lot of hope.

> "HAVE A PLAN—AND A
> LOT OF HOPE."

Let the Company See You Are on Its Side

"One of the basic causes for all the trouble in the world today is that people talk too much and think too little. They act impulsively without thinking. I always try to think before I talk."

Margaret Chase Smith, the first woman elected to both the U.S. House of Representatives and the U.S. Senate

To let the company see you are on its side you need to do some concrete things, such as the following:

- Buy some stock in the company.
- Read the company newsletter—better still, edit the damn thing.
- Support company functions.
- Show an interest.
- Ask questions.
- Have your interest in the company noticed and recorded in some way.
- Focus on what you contribute to the company, not on what you get out of it.
- Use the company's products or services.
- Actively speak well of the company.
- Rehearse saying what you think is good about the company— have a ready answer at hand if asked.
- Know the company's mission statement and philosophy.
- Know the company's products and/or services inside and out.

- Know the company history—its formation, its mergers and acquisitions etc., its long-term goals and its key personnel (founder etc.).
- Know the company's social standing and what it does for the community.

What you do not do—*ever*—is bad-mouth the company, under any circumstances.

"But, but, but," I hear you say, "Won't this make me out to be a yes-person, a lackey, a company mouthpiece?" Nope. Not if you do it right. If you talk platitudes and seem insincere, people will know it is an act and that you are a company pawn. But if you are strong about it people will take your lead and follow suit. Set an example. Be outspoken in your praise for the company. It is such an unfashionable thing to do you will make your mark, but you do have to be sincere and bold.

"But what if I don't feel so good about the company?" Then get out. It's a two-way process. They employ you. You work for them. You give and they give. You take and they take. If you're unhappy about this relationship, then get out, get a divorce, find another lover. You have to love your company and see it as a relationship. If you're in a bad one, what are you going to do about it? Put up and shut up? I hope not.

> ## "SET AN EXAMPLE. BE OUTSPOKEN IN YOUR PRAISE FOR THE COMPANY."

Don't Bad-Mouth your Boss

"Kill my boss? Do I dare live out the American dream?"

Homer Simpson

Okay, so your boss is a jerk and you can't stand working under such a weasel and you've just got to tell everyone you meet what a fool this boss is. Yes? No. Wrong, wrong, wrong. You do not bad-mouth your boss under any circumstances. Okay, so your whole team knows your boss is useless and they make that clear to you. Do you agree? No, you do not. Never, ever. If you can't find anything good to say, then say nothing at all. You do not put them down even if they deserve it, or you feel they do anyway.

Your boss is your boss. If they are that dreadful, then don't work for them, go look someplace else. If you are going to work for them, then that is your choice and you have to stick with it, live with it, support it, believe in it—or you'll go crazy.

> "IF YOU CAN'T FIND ANYTHING GOOD TO SAY, THEN SAY NOTHING AT ALL."

RULE 76

If your boss is a nightmare, it is your job to turn that around. Get them to trust you. Then get them to delegate to you. Then get them to hand over responsibility to you. Then replace them. Simple, isn't it? Obviously not, but these are the steps you must take if you are serious and committed.

Watch what you say about your boss in case it gets back to their boss—who might just happen to be a fan of your boss and not take kindly to you bad-mouthing them. After all, they put them there and for you to publicly question that decision leaves you in a precarious situation yourself.

I once worked for a complete son of a . . . who drank, kept bad company, and didn't know if it was New York or New Year most of the time. Someone complained about him to headquarters and a team was sent down to take statements. Twelve junior managers, including myself, were questioned about his behavior. I refused to cooperate and said nothing. A year later my boss was still there and I was still there, but 11 other junior managers no longer worked for that company. Moral: Keep quiet if you can't be nice. How come he survived? Beats me. He obviously had connections in the right places. How did I survive? No idea. He trusted me and I kept my head down and got on with my job; his behavior didn't affect me unduly and I coped.

Don't Bad-Mouth Your Team

> "Tact is the ability to describe others as they see themselves."
>
> Eleanor Chaffee

So you can't bad-mouth the company and you can't put down your boss. "Surely," I hear you ask, "I can criticize my team?" Not in public you can't. Behind closed doors when there is no one there but you and you alone, then and only then are you allowed one small silent scream when things really hit the fan, but apart from that, nothing.

It's a poor work person who blames their tools. Your team is your tool to getting your management job done. If your team is useless it is you who hasn't sharpened the tool, oiled it, cleaned the rust off, repaired the handle, replaced worn out bits, checked for damage, that sort of thing.

Your team will make mistakes, that's a given. Things will go wrong, that too is a given. You're dealing with people; they screw up from time to time, get emotional, let you down, fail to work as a team, goof off, and generally behave completely normally. You'd be a fool not to expect this, to plan for it, to build it into your plans. Look, things go wrong and criticizing your team doesn't help. Learn from it and move on.

You have to "publicly celebrate those who move the organization closer to the attainment of its vision and strategic goal"—that's your team. If you criticize your team, you are focusing on the

> ## "THINGS GO WRONG AND CRITICIZING YOUR TEAM DOESN'T HELP. LEARN FROM IT AND MOVE ON."

negative, which will spiral them downward. If you praise them, it's an uplifting experience.

If you critizcizing your team, you are putting yourself down and admitting publicly you are a bad manager. Don't do it—you're not.

Accept That Some Things Bosses Tell You to Do Will Be Wrong

"I find it rather easy to portray a businessman. Being bland, rather cruel, and incompetent comes naturally to me."

John Cleese

Just because you do your job well doesn't mean everyone else does. Some bosses are useless and there's no getting away from that. Sometimes they will tell you to do stuff that is crazy. Sometimes they will issue orders that are so obviously off the wall you can't help but gasp. Sometimes they will tell you to do things that are completely wrong. What are you to do? You have various options:

* Refuse
* Leave
* Seek advice from your union/management advisory body/ trade body if you are on one
* Ask for advice from human resources
* Ask for advice from other managers
* Ask for advice from your boss's boss
* Put your concerns in writing
* Do it but grumble a lot

- Do it with a cheerful smile and a whistle
- Talk to your boss about your misgivings

Initially it might be politic to go and talk to your boss in person, face to face, over an informal coffee; a bit of a chat, nothing too heavy. Point out that you think you have a problem with their order. Don't make it personal. Don't attack them. Don't tell them they are crap. Explain that it is you that has the problem. The order and your boss are fine but you feel uncomfortable. Put the ball firmly back in their lap. If they insist, end by saying you still feel uncomfortable about it and would like time to seek further advice. Ask if you can put your fears in writing and whether they would do the same.

Sometimes you have to accept that bosses don't know what they are doing, ain't going to change, and you have to put up with it. Or you could simply refuse or leave. Your call. The Rule is that you should accept that it happens from time to time.

> "SOMETIMES YOU HAVE TO ACCEPT THAT BOSSES DON'T KNOW WHAT THEY ARE DOING."

Accept That Bosses Are as Scared as You Are at Times

"If you're not the lead dog, the scenery never changes."

Bumper sticker

Poor things, they too get frightened, paranoid, lost, feel unloved, confused, at sea, vulnerable, and alone. Your job is to take away your bosses' pain, their fears, and make them relax.

You are a manager and have to manage not only downward but upward as well. When you deal with your bosses you mustn't ever do the following:

* Threaten
* Usurp
* Intimidate
* Pressure
* Menace
* Disrespect
* Question (apart from under Rule 78)
* Undermine
* Ridicule

RULE 79

Instead you have to support, back, encourage, comfort, console, cheer up, relieve the pressure on, be utterly dependable, take the strain, guard the fort, and eventually perhaps replace them—with yourself, of course.

Some bosses are so stricken with panic they are incapable of making decisions. You will have to make decisions for them and reassure them that everything is fine—the nurse is here now and they can go and lie down.

> "YOUR JOB IS TO TAKE AWAY YOUR BOSSES' PAIN, THEIR FEARS, AND MAKE THEM RELAX."

Avoid Straitjacket Thinking

"No one is less ready for tomorrow than the person who holds the most rigid beliefs about what tomorrow will contain."

Watts Wacker, Jim Taylor, and Howard Means,
The Visionary's Handbook

When you've got your head down and things are flying at you from all directions, it is easy to forget that you are supposed to be an innovative, creative, cutting-edge sort of manager. We all do it. We get so close to the work under our noses we lose sight of the fact that we *can* invent, inspire, lead, motivate—and say "Yes." The team comes to you with a new idea and you are so weary from fighting the bureaucracy, the system, the weather, and the commuting that you just say "No," no matter what it is they are suggesting. It's often a "No" with a subtext of "And leave me alone, I'm too busy/stressed/irritable to think about this now." Is that you? Bet it is sometimes. It's all of us.

So, we need to throw the straitjacket off. We need to lift our heads. We need to consider the options and think "Why not?" and "What *would* happen if we did this?" We need to stop being constrained by pressure and by work.

An easy way out of the straitjacket is to consider how you would view your job, your department, or your team if you were a stranger coming in from the outside, coming in to do your job for the very first time. What would you change? What would you

> ## "IT IS EASY TO FORGET THAT YOU ARE SUPPOSED TO BE AN INNOVATIVE, CREATIVE, CUTTING-EDGE SORT OF MANAGER."

leave alone? Think of what you're doing from the point of view of your customers—what makes sense? What doesn't?

It is too easy to get so bogged down in minutiae that we fail to stand back and look at things with fresh eyes every day. But if we are to be the best sort of manager ever to roam the earth, we must stay fresh or go the way of the dinosaurs. Staying fresh means being open to new ideas, new suggestions, new concepts, and new directions.

RULE 81

Act and Talk As If You Are One of *Them*

"My mother said to me, "If you become a soldier, you'll be a general; if you become a monk, you'll end up as the Pope." Instead, I became a painter and wound up as Picasso."

Pablo Picasso

Okay, before you actually *become* one of them, you should be *practicing* to become one of them. If you are a junior manager, you should be studying the way middle managers walk and talk and be ready to become one. If you are a middle manager, you should be acting and talking as if you were already a senior manager. And on, right up to the top.

> "IF YOU ARE A MIDDLE MANAGER, YOU SHOULD BE ACTING AND TALKING AS IF YOU WERE ALREADY A SENIOR MANAGER."

RULE 81

When I first became a managing director of a company, I almost forgot this Rule. I carried on managing as if I was a senior manager. But sales weren't going as well as I would have liked. I was organizing corporate sales and couldn't get to talk to the right people. I read somewhere that kings only talk to kings. I became a king. (Substitute "managing director" for "king" and you'll see what I mean.) Immediately doors which previously had been closed were opened and sales exceeded my expectations.

If you're going to be a king in the future, you had better start practicing now. Watch how anyone senior to you does things. The way they answer the phone, talk to staff, what they wear, what paper they read, how they get to work, what they do at work, and how they do it.

I recently met a managing director of a very large company and I was seriously impressed with how friendly and informal he was with his staff—who obviously adored him—and how genuinely relaxed he seemed. That is until we came to negotiate, when he was obviously totally up on his job and had facts and figures at his fingertips in a second. I watched him because he is my next step, if you like. He is my "one of them."

And no, no matter how high you go, you never walk on people—ever.

Show You Understand the Viewpoint of Underlings *and* Overlings

"Courtesy toward opponents and eagerness to understand their viewpoint is the ABC of nonviolence."

Mahatma Gandhi

Being an underling—as we all know because we've all done it, been there—is tough. You get to take a lot of orders from a lot of people delivered in a way that makes you defensive and makes you angry.

But hey, being a manager is often no better. Now you are caught in the middle. You get all that flack from the staff, plus all the crazy directives from the chief executive. You are no longer an underling and not quite an overling. You are the middle of the sandwich. You're going to get it from both directions, upward and downward.

One of the best ways to take the pressure off is to let them all know you understand their viewpoint. Don't just smile and say, "Yeah, I know where you're coming from," when it is plainly obvious you don't. You really have to make sure they know you do understand their needs and wants, grievances and demands, and fears and hopes. Up and down the chain.

When push comes to shove you are going to have to side with the overlings sometimes. When you think they are right, of course. Your underlings—non-PC for team—will obviously resent this, particularly as they will not welcome any change (especially ones they don't understand). This is a good time to let them tell you how they feel and tell them that you do understand this, and explain why the overlings have decided to do what they have.

If you're really good, one day you'll learn to explain how the underlings perceive things to the overlings, in terms they will understand—and vice versa. If you can get the underlings to see why the overlings believe that something is not in their best interests makes sense, then you're on the road to becoming a managerial genius.

> "ONE OF THE BEST WAYS
> TO TAKE THE PRESSURE
> OFF IS TO LET THEM ALL
> KNOW YOU UNDERSTAND
> THEIR VIEWPOINT."

Don't Back Down—Be Prepared to Stand Your Ground

"Whoever the villain in your life is, don't be afraid to confront them."

www.effective meetings.com

There will be times when you are certain and know you're right. In these times, sometimes you have to make a stand. You have to be prepared to put up or shut up. You have to be prepared to fight for what you believe in. If you are passionate about what you do, then standing up for what you know is right isn't that hard.

You don't have to be aggressive, just resolute. If you are being bullied, say so loud and clear—chances are the person harassing you will back off, quick.

> "IF YOU ARE PASSIONATE ABOUT WHAT YOU DO, THEN STANDING UP FOR WHAT YOU KNOW IS RIGHT ISN'T THAT HARD."

You don't have to be rude, just assertive. If someone is spreading rumors about you or your team or your performance that aren't true, then manage them. State your position clearly: "I hear you are spreading such and such a rumor. This is not true and I would appreciate it if you would stop."

You don't have to be angry, just be very certain of yourself and very well prepared. If someone always finds fault with what you suggest, such as "Oh, that won't work, we tried it before and it failed," then stand your ground and don't back down. Say, "Yes, and here are the figures to show why it didn't work. And here is my report to explain why it will work this time and how it is different."

You don't have to get fired, just fired up. If you work for a boss who fails to give you suitable feedback, keep plugging away. Ask, "How can I improve my performance for next time? What steps should I take to get that pay raise I want that you've just said no to? Where do you see me in a year's time? What can we do to improve sales?" Keep pushing the ball back into their court until they are forced to give you suitable answers.

You don't have to be argumentative, just conciliatory. If you have a boss suggesting you cut legal corners, don't point-blank refuse and cause an argument. Instead say, "Ah. How would we handle this if the media/auditors got hold of it?" You aren't refusing but you are standing your ground and not going along with their ideas—and you are also offering them a way out. They won't have to make a point and impose their will on you, but they can now diplomatically back down without losing face.

> ## "YOU DON'T HAVE TO GET
> ## FIRED, JUST FIRED UP."

RULE 84

Don't Play Politics

"If you're in a meeting and someone is playing politics, just say to them: 'You're playing politics, come back when you feel better'."

Sir John Harvey-Jones, former managing director of ICI

Politicians are people paid to play politics. You are not. You are a manager. You manage situations and projects. The people don't need managing. They manage themselves. Some of them get off track sometimes and play politics. You don't have to play with them. That's like playing on the tracks. You're bound to get hurt, bound to get run over by a train. Playing politics is using people to further your own ends, which, if you are playing politics properly, will be unpleasant, selfish, narrow-minded, and petty. Playing politics invariably involves intimidating people, being sly, getting things done by lying or other dishonest means, not being yourself or true to others and generally behaving appallingly. There, I've said it now and I guess you know what I think of playing politics—it stinks.

You should "love thy neighbor, but pick thy neighborhood." Try to hang out with people who don't feel the need to play politics.

Try to be involved with less-popular projects because they attract less attention, less competition. Same goes for the less-popular team or department. Here you can shine without having to compete all the time. Every company has people who get stuff done without backstabbing. Hang out with these people.

Share information, always. This takes the wind out of the sails of those who do play politics. Be everyone's friend so no one can accuse you of being cliquey or stand-offish.

> "EVERY COMPANY HAS
> PEOPLE WHO GET STUFF
> DONE WITHOUT
> BACKSTABBING. HANG OUT
> WITH THESE PEOPLE."

Although you aren't going to play, you still have to be on your guard—aware that playing politics goes on and be ready to deal with it in an appropriate way. Watch out for the hidden agendas that go on, the concealing of true motives, the smear campaigns, the lying, the gossip (often malicious), the hints and subtle nuances that you aren't up to scratch or speed, the jockeying for power and control, the whispering—that sort of thing. If you are fortunate, you will encounter very little of it and any you do can be cut off quickly. Some industries seem to breed that sort of bad behavior and you will find it difficult to stop it. Refuse to play, and get a reputation for being a straight-talking, unpolitical being— honest, above board, open, candid, guileless, and straightforward. Nothing complicated about you.

Don't Put Down Other Managers

> "It has always been the prerogative of children and half-wits to point out that the emperor has no clothes. But the half-wit remains a half-wit, and the emperor remains an emperor."
>
> Neil Gaiman and Marc Hempel, *The Sandman: The Kindly Ones*

Earlier we looked at how competition should spur you on, encourage you, and how you should never be frightened of it. We were talking about the competition of other industries, other organizations. But what of colleagues and other departments? Same goes. Don't be frightened of anyone or anything. If you are good at what you do, bold, creative, fast on your feet—as I am sure you are—then there is no need. If you refuse to engage in politics, then you will be seen as honest and trustworthy. You should never criticize, make inferences about, put down, condemn, pass judgement on, or whine about your colleagues or people from other departments/divisions.

If you do, you will be seen as weak or a poor performer. Sure, others will, and will be seen to profit from it at times. But do they sleep at night? Can they, hand on heart, swear they enjoy their job, or do they fear others betraying them as they have betrayed others? I think not. I've worked with quite a few. They go on about how good they are, how bad everyone else is, but they quake in their boots privately because deep down they know they aren't as good at their jobs as those whom they criticize. Just because someone points out your faults doesn't make you any less of an

> ## "IF YOU REFUSE TO ENGAGE IN POLITICS, THEN YOU WILL BE SEEN AS HONEST AND TRUSTWORTHY."

emperor, does it? And if you see another emperor with their new clothes, there is no point in pointing it out to them that they have been fooled—no one will thank you.

I worked with one manager who would bang on incessantly about all the other managers and how bad they were. Interesting thing was every fault he pointed out, he was equally guilty of. We laughed because it was so obvious to everyone but him. He couldn't see he was highlighting his own faults.

Share What You Know

"Share what you know and, more importantly, what you imagine with others. Lead them to discover their own truths. The way you live your life is as powerful a teaching for others as what you say to them."

Tom Cowan, shamanic practitioner

This Rule is about mentoring people who know less than you. They don't have to know that much less, and you don't have to know that much more. But if you share everything you do know, then they will know as much as you. Some managers will see this as a threat. They are the foolish ones. What you have just done is train up someone to take some of the workload from your shoulders. Someone to replace you when you get promoted.

Some managers feel awkward about sharing because they feel they don't know enough. But when you learned English at school, it was enough that your teacher knew about grammar and clauses and punctuation and that sort of stuff. You didn't need an award-winning novelist or a Nobel Prize winner. No, just a humble English teacher was enough.

Sharing with colleagues is important too. The more you give out, the more you'll get back. Suppose you give one bit of information to 20 other managers. If only half of them are generous enough to return the favor, it means you now have 10 bits of new information to add to your collection. They have only gained by one but you have gained by 10—easy. They will invariably share with you, but not each other—don't ask me why. Perhaps they feel indebted to you and not to them.

Don't Intimidate

"In order to keep a true perspective of one's importance, everyone should have a dog that will worship him and a cat that will ignore him."

Dereke Bruce

Being a manager gives you authority and power, no doubt about that. Perhaps that's what separates good managers like you from bad ones. You know how to handle that power and you don't abuse it.

People will look up to you as a manager, respect you, and even fear you. You have the power of unemployment or work over them, and they will be aware of that in all their dealings with you. But you have to try and overcome that by getting them to trust you. Always be predictable so that they know where they are with you at all times and you don't frighten them by taking them by surprise. You mustn't abuse your position by intimidating your team.

Yes, there are two ways of getting things done—fear and reward—and a lot of managers choose the first because they feel under-confident, unsure, and uncertain. Unlike you, they aren't at ease with themselves, and this shows up in a threatening or bullying attitude toward their staff. We ought to pity them—or, if we work under such a boss ourselves, try and get them better trained. Perhaps leave a copy of this book lying around for them to stumble on accidentally?

A lot of managers don't know that their attitude sets the standard for how their staff treats each other and their customers. If they see a manager who is kind and cooperative, rewarding to work for, and confident, it rubs off, and they, in turn, act the same way toward each other and toward customers as well.

Working this way makes life easier and more productive. It's so much better to work in an organization where reward is used instead of fear to get things done.

> "IT'S SO MUCH BETTER TO WORK IN AN ORGANIZATION WHERE REWARD IS USED INSTEAD OF FEAR TO GET THINGS DONE."

Be Above Interdepartmental Warfare

"If there had been investigations, which there haven't, or not necessarily, or I'm not at liberty to say whether there have, there would have been a project team which, had it existed, on which I cannot comment, would now have been disbanded, if it had existed, and the members returned to their original departments, if indeed there had been any such members."

Sir Humphrey in *Yes Minister*

I once worked for two bosses at the same time. They were directors of the company, and they hated each other. Each had an agenda. Each fought a vicious campaign against the other with us managers—and staff—as their foot soldiers, pawns, cannon fodder. It wasn't pleasant. They had their own area of responsibility, and if you worked solely in any such area you were happy, because you had one boss. But if you, like me, had to cross over frequently from one director's area into the other's, then life was made intolerable. The two directors countermanded each other's orders, played dirty tricks on each other, wouldn't speak to each other, and generally behaved like very small children. I learned, and learned fast, to be a diplomat and a tactician. One director worked upstairs and one downstairs. I was sent up and down and learned to stop on the landing half way and stay there until each had forgotten what particular bit of interdepartmental warfare was going on. I also learned to play them off each other to get what I wanted—but that was not very nice.

I guess that was about as bad as it got, but I've also worked in companies where the rivalry between departments was extreme and interfered with productivity, kept staff on edge, and contributed, I think, to very high staff turnover. You would have thought the directors would have stopped it, but in my first example you would see that even directors are capable of being very silly and childish. Don't you go the same way. Steer clear of it, if you want my advice. Be open and honest and up-front in all your dealings, and then you will earn a good reputation and no one will be able to accuse you of being underhanded.

> "EVEN DIRECTORS ARE
> CAPABLE OF BEING VERY
> SILLY AND CHILDISH."

Show That You'll Fight to the Death for Your Team

"Jim: Who else is in this department?

Sir Humphrey: Well briefly, sir, I am the Permanent Undersecretary of State known as the Permanent Secretary, Wooley here is your Principle Private Secretary. I too have a Principle Private Secretary, and he is the Principle Private Secretary to the Permanent Secretary. Directly responsible to me are 10 Deputy Secretaries, 87 Undersecretaries and 219 Assistant Secretaries. Directly responsible to the Principle Private Secretaries are Plain Private Secretaries, and the Prime Minister will be appointing two Parliamentary Undersecretaries and you will be appointing your own Parliamentary Private Secretary.

Jim: Can they all type?

Sir Humphrey: None of us can type, Minister. Mrs. McKay types, she's the secretary."

Yes Minister

Your team is your tool for getting the job done—whatever it happens to be. Without your team—and that can be one lone person or thousands of people—you are nothing. Without your team, you are an empty page waiting to be written—or typed. You must support your team, praise it, fight for it—to the death if need be. The brilliant manager—we don't need to say who that is by now, do we?—generates loyalty and respect by being the team cheerleader—that's you.

You have to make people on your team see that you are not only their mentor, leader, guardian, and protector, but also their champion, their hero, their defender. If anyone tries to criticize them, you will rise to their defense. If anyone tries to take advantage of them, you will rush to protect them.

On the other hand, you could always throw them to the wolves. See how far it gets you. But there are a lot of managers out there who seem to think that's the clever option, the right choice. What do you think? I've worked for and with some, and believe me they lose staff so fast.

If your staff have seen you defend them once, they will know they can trust you to have their best interests at heart. They'll know that if something unfair is being imposed on them, you will stand up for them. This also means that if you accept something, they are likely to accept it, too—which makes for a smoother life all around.

> "WITHOUT YOUR TEAM,
> YOU ARE AN EMPTY PAGE
> WAITING TO BE
> WRITTEN."

Aim for Respect Rather Than Being Liked

"It is a given that all students will not be attracted to all teachers. It is also a given that respect,
rather than being liked, is the hallmark of great
teachers. But chances of achieving both are far
greater through encouragement and empower-
ment than by saying, "Call me by my first name."

Dr. Marvin Marshall, *Promoting Learning*

Don't you just hate the manager who tries to be your friend, one
of the guys/girls, your pal. We've all worked with them, and they
are a mess. They embarrass themselves as much as their team.
Aim for aloof. Aim for respect rather than being liked. Look, you
want your staff to give you all they've got, not hugs and drinks at
the bar. You want them to think you're a god, not someone who
needs everyone's affirmation.

> "YOU HAVE TO CREATE
> MYSTIQUE, AN AIR OF
> POWER."

RULE 90

You have to create mystique, an air of power, authority, friendliness, without the desperate need to be liked. You have to remain detached.

Someday you may have to fire some of these people, and you don't need to make it any tougher on yourself than you have to.

Someday you will have to promote some of these people, and you don't want to be seen as having favorites.

They've got to be able to look up to you, respect you, have you as a role model. They can't do that if you've been seen rolling around on the floor of the bar drunk as a skunk on a Friday evening, now can they? You can't create mystique if you try to be too friendly with them. Maintain a distance, and they won't see it as standoffishness, but will respect the space you give them.

Maintain a physical aloofness as well: no backslapping, hugging, kissing, hair ruffling (hey, I had a manager who used to do this to me; I hated it and him—I was very young but that shouldn't have made any difference), arm wrestling (you could lose and you'd lose all respect then, believe me), office football, or any form of rough-housing. Maintain your dignity at all times—and your style, credibility, sanity, and authority.

Do One or Two Things Well and Avoid the Rest

"The first 90 percent of a project takes 90 percent of the time. The last 10 percent takes the other 90 percent of the time."

Anonymous

The really good manager is a specialist. You can't do everything. You can't do everyone's job. You can't do more than a few things each day anyway. It's best to pick your specialist subject, be really, really good at it, and leave the rest to other people. In my company, we have a very clear demarcation of who does what. I try to do as little as possible. I figure the better the manager, the less you do; it's all down to your powers of delegation.

> "BEST TO PICK YOUR SPECIALIST SUBJECT, BE REALLY, REALLY GOOD AT IT, AND LEAVE THE REST TO OTHER PEOPLE."

So I stick to what I do best, which is basically talking to other managers. I don't do sales, but I do open doors for sales staff to walk through. I don't do key accounts, but I do set up contacts for our key contact people to follow through. I don't do accounts, but I do oversee the accounting staff. My "one or two things" is setting up meetings for my team to do the business, and overseeing the overall style of the company—its branding, its corporate identity, its place in the market. I manage the company, but I don't do products. I know my limitations. I know what I am good at and what I am bad at. I'm lousy on detail, routine, order, regular everyday stuff. I am good on sudden, unorthodox, interesting, one-off, people-orientated projects. I don't see what I am good at as being better, nor do I see the things I am bad at as being inferior. Quite the opposite, in fact. I envy the ordered, those who can pay attention to detail, those who like to see a project through from beginning to end, those with empty in-baskets and tidy desks.

What are you good at? And bad? How would you best describe the one or two things you could do well?

Seek Feedback on Your Performance

"It is better to have enough ideas for some of them to be wrong, than to be always right by having no ideas at all."

Edward de Bono, lateral thinker

Usually we don't go around seeking approval because we can follow our gut instincts and we know when we have done a good job. But feedback is always a good thing. You should seek feedback from your peers, your rivals, your team, your bosses, and your customers. You are not seeking praise, approval, or love, merely feedback. Remember you are all on the same team—from the janitor right up to the CEO, all kicking toward the same goal, all waving the same flag—or should be.

You should seek feedback to

- Identify your strengths and weaknesses.
- Compare the feedback with your own assessment of any situation—to make sure you are on track and realistic with your own self-appraisal.
- Learn from a situation where you went wrong—or got it right—for next time.
- Identify problem areas that need action and over which you have responsibility.
- See how your team is performing—as additional information to your own assessment.

See, none of this involves praise or approval (or love). It is a realistic appraisal of a situation or project so you can learn and move on.

Now, how do you ask for feedback? Well, asking people in the team is easy. "So, team, how did we do?" They'll tell you, all right.

Next, your boss. "So, Boss, how did I do?" Again easy.

Customers? Easy. "Is there anything we could do to improve the service / product / delivery times / specifications / proposal?" They'll tell you, as well.

Colleagues? Just ask. "So, could you give me some feedback on how you saw the relocation go off?" Or, "Could you tell me how you think we (you and your team) did with the exhibition?" Or, "Any chance of some feedback on the cost-cutting exercise / new accounting procedure / staffing levels over the summer vacations / new theme park ride?" Don't preface it with, "Can you tell me where I went wrong?" or, "I know the relocation went off appallingly, but I don't know where we screwed up." Or, even worse, "Help me out here, can you? I done wrong, but no one will tell me what I did." Don't give anyone your judgment of the situation in advance. Let them tell you the good and the bad. Just nod at it all and say, "Thank you" and move on.

> "LET THEM TELL YOU THE GOOD AND THE BAD. JUST NOD AT IT ALL AND SAY 'THANK YOU' AND MOVE ON."

Maintain Good Relationships and Friendships

"Don't flatter yourself that friendship authorizes you to say disagreeable things to your intimates. The nearer you come into relation with a person, the more necessary do tact and courtesy become."

Oliver Wendell Holmes, American poet

I have a friend who has a catchphrase—don't we all?—and his is, "I don't see how that can possibly be good manners." He uses it if anyone interrupts him at meetings or steals his ideas. I love it because it says everything about poor working relationships. Good manners—what a simple concept but how big a subject.

It is easy to maintain good relationships and friendships at work if you maintain good manners. This doesn't have to mean opening doors for people or carrying their briefcases. Good manners means being polite, warm, human, compassionate, helpful, welcoming—all the things you'd be for your customers, or should be. (I'm sure you are.)

This becomes tricky when it comes to somebody you don't like, have clashed with in the past, or who has been rude or unpleasant to you. But that's when it's most important to use this skill.

RULE 93

Even the rudest and most unpleasant person will find it very hard to keep being rude if you are pleasant, smiling, and open with them (especially if you can bear to throw in a little flattery about their expertise on a subject—if it's justified, of course).

Try to see your colleagues as if they were equally warm as yourself. If you always approach everyone with cheerful optimism, you'll find that they simply have no choice but to respond in kind. Offer help when you can. Speak to everyone as if they were your equal—as indeed they are. Look for the positive points in people—find something to like or respect about them and focus on that. Take as much time with the most modest of employees as you would with the highest. Treat everyone the same—with respect and decency.

> "IF YOU ALWAYS APPROACH EVERYONE WITH CHEERFUL OPTIMISM, YOU'LL FIND THAT THEY SIMPLY HAVE NO CHOICE BUT TO RESPOND IN KIND."

Build Respect—Both Ways—Between You and Your Customers

"Each of us should know what our customers expect before they know it."

Dinesh K. Gupta and Ashok Jambhekar

I was listening to a double-talking salesperson on the radio the other day, and the way he was talking about his customers made me think he and they were different species. He was condescending, patronizing, abusive, belittling, and ridiculing. He seemed to think it was fair to con people—he said it was up to us to check the small print, and if we didn't we were somehow stupid. I have no respect for such people because of these attitudes—and the fact that they phone me most evenings as I sit down to dinner with my children. I have a whole range of techniques to punish them for this, including pretending to be deaf and making them shout, saying they need to speak to my father and leaving the phone off the hook until they get bored and hang up.

Don't cheat or lie to your customers. You need them. It's a two-way street and it is an important relationship. Customers are never too much trouble. They provide my food and clothing and nice car and good vacations. Why should I abuse them? In return, I provide them with entertainment, fun, quality products, a brand they can be proud of, a lifestyle they can buy into, and a sense of belonging to an exciting and dynamic company. I respect them for what they give me, and they respect me for what I give them.

> "DON'T CHEAT OR LIE TO YOUR CUSTOMERS. YOU NEED THEM."

Go the Extra Mile for Your Customers

"Brilliance is a standard, not a skill."

Michael Heppell, *How to Be Brilliant*

This is the easiest rule of all. Going the extra mile should be the first thing on your mind when you wake in the morning and the last thing at night. Everything you do should be to take service that bit further. The trouble is, customers are such a pain in the backside. They want stuff, they demand, they are difficult, they complain, they call at unnatural hours, they expect service above and beyond, they think the whole damn business should be run for them, they moan when we move our call center to India, they want money off, free gifts, two for one, buy one get one free, money back if they are dissatisfied, replacement products, guarantees, safety checks, harmless products. God, who do they think they are? Strike a chord here? Ring any bells? I've worked in industries where the customer wasn't so much king as an inconvenience.

Let's clear up one thing here and now. Without the customer there is no point. No point coming in. No point making anything. No point creating anything. No point doing anything. Without the customer, we are all flying blind.

Okay, point made. Now that we realize the importance of customers, we have to think of ways of getting them, keeping them, satisfying them, welcoming them, going the extra mile for them. We don't have to kiss up to them, but we do have to be creative in the ways we woo them. It's a lot cheaper to service an existing customer than to recruit a new one. Keep the ones you've got by being nice to them. Quick exercise: Think of three ways of going the extra mile for your customer right now.

> ## "WITHOUT THE CUSTOMER, WE ARE ALL FLYING BLIND."

Be Aware of Your Responsibilities and Stick to Your Principles

"Success is not the key to happiness. Happiness is the key to success. If you love what you are doing, you will be successful."

Albert Schweitzer

As a manager, you have a responsibility to people on your team. You must make sure they don't come to harm while they are in your care. You have to make sure they are safe, healthy, cared for, well fed and watered, comfortable, kept well away from hazardous substances and equipment, and that they wear suitable safety clothing if necessary.

Now you also have a responsibility to the environment in much the same way. You mustn't do anything that is going to do harm, cause lasting damage, put anyone at risk of health or life, or cause any land to be utilized in a worse way than it was before you came along. You don't have to be an eco-warrior, but you do have a responsibility not to cause harm or damage. Can you put your hand on your heart and say your managerial role is "clean"?

You have to have some principles—that you won't cause harm or damage. There has to be a line drawn—by you—somewhere, beyond which you will not go. You have to give something back. You have to be aware of what is going on around you. You have to be aware of what your industry contributes—or takes—from the environment.

> ## "CAN YOU PUT YOUR HAND ON YOUR HEART AND SAY YOUR MANAGERIAL ROLE IS 'CLEAN'?"

This isn't stuff from the fairies or the hippies or the karmic religionists—this is real stuff. The more you put in, the more you get out. Be good and sleep nights. It's not a bad philosophy to live by and to manage with.

Be Straight at All Times and Speak the Truth

"I have found that being honest is the best technique I can use. Right up front, tell people what you're trying to accomplish and what you're willing to sacrifice to accomplish it."

Lee Iacocca, former president of Ford and of Chrysler

This rule follows right on from the previous rule. Obviously if you think your boss is an idiot, you don't go and tell him—that's taking honesty just a bit too far. But don't lie, or cheat, or steal, or abuse, or defraud, or take advantage, or con, or trick, or swindle, or hinder, or worsen.

As a manager, you have been given a privileged position—one of trust and honor. You are responsible for human lives—no, really, real human lives. You screw up and people get hurt. When your

> "AS A MANAGER YOU HAVE BEEN GIVEN A PRIVILEGED POSITION – ONE OF TRUST AND HONOR."

employees go home after working for you all day, they carry on living and breathing, feeling and loving, hurting and dreaming and hoping. If you upset them or offend them or abuse them or lie to them, they take that home and it affects their close family, friends, and relatives. You must speak truth to them at all times. If you can't say anything nice, say nothing, but don't lie.

Don't lie to your bosses. They don't employ you to do that. They employ you to be straight and to tell the truth. If you're not going to make your figures, don't fudge the issue—tell them. They can then take measures to help you or take action because your not making your figures might have additional effects. They might be let down, but they will be grateful for the warning. Better to know than to hope and be disappointed.

Don't lie to customers. Obviously in all this there is a measure for artistic truth telling. If a customer asks if your products are superior to your competitors, you don't have to lie because they are—or you'd be working for the competition, wouldn't you? But if they ask if certain products have been successful and they haven't, you are entitled to creative truth telling. Say, "We have been somewhat surprised by sales so far, but there is always room for improvement," rather than, "These really bombed, but we're hoping you'll take a load off our hands."

Don't Cut Corners— You'll Get Caught

"Do you ever compromise on service? Do you cut corners, only partially fulfil, or even forget commitments? Exceptional service means keeping every commitment you make to customers. Period."

Mark Sanborn, motivational speaker

Maybe you make airplanes—are you going to cut corners? Maybe use substandard metal in the wings? Replace the engines with junkyard replacements? I don't think so. You'd get caught pretty quick. Hey, there is an increasing trend of taking managers to court if they have been responsible for injury to anyone using one of their products that has been found to be faulty (by way of design or manufacture or cost cutting). Fair enough. If we are all made to be personally responsible for what we do in our working lives, maybe things would be a whole lot better.

Maybe you don't make airplanes. Maybe you don't make anything. Maybe you just program computers. Nice and safe. Can't hurt anyone there, can you? No? Sure? Think things through. Work out worst-case scenarios and be prepared for the fact that whatever we do as managers, we are responsible for someone or something that could get damaged, hurt, wounded, upset, impaired, killed—you name it.

Cutting corners isn't worth it—you'll always get caughtt. Sod's law. I know you can get caught between the devil and the deep blue sea at times, with your boss telling you to do something and your principles telling you it is madness, but you need the job, and the mortgage has to be paid, and it's easier to shut up and pretend it's all right. But it isn't. You'll get caught.

> ## "IF WE ARE ALL MADE TO BE PERSONALLY RESPONSIBLE FOR WHAT WE DO IN OUR WORKING LIVES, MAYBE THINGS WOULD BE A WHOLE LOT BETTER."

And you have to move heaven and earth to prove to your boss that cutting corners is a real waste of time. The old, "But what would the media/auditors make of this if they got hold of it?" argument often works wonders. As does asking about what insurance we carry or how the legal department has viewed this cost-cutting exercise. If you are told, "I haven't bothered running it past them," you can clap your hand to your head and shriek, "Oh, no, I'm working with a crazy person." Using humor can get someone else to realize they have overstepped the mark and need to think.

Be In Command and Take Charge

"It is acknowledged that many leaders do not have empathy, but it is observed that those who lack empathy lack the ability to move people. Leaders who can instill an atmosphere of working together gain respect, taking charge without taking control."

Warren Bennis, *On Becoming a Leader*

You are a manager, so manage. Managing means just that, managing. Managing to work effectively. Managing to be in charge. Managing to be in command.

There seems to be a new movement in which managers are frightened to take command. They seem reluctant to assume control in case their team might resent this or accuse them of being a dictator. Nothing could be further from the truth. Teams with good, strong, commanding managers go a lot further because they know there is a captain at the helm. Without a captain we are all at sea—lost, scared, about to crash on the rocks. In a way, it almost doesn't matter what captain we've got, just so long as we've got someone with their hand on the rudder. We all know the first mate does all the real sailing anyway, so the captain can be whatever, but the first mate can't function unless they know there is someone there, at the helm.

> ## "TEAMS WITH GOOD, STRONG, COMMANDING MANAGERS GO A LOT FURTHER BECAUSE THEY KNOW THERE IS A CAPTAIN AT THE HELM."

You've got to be a hero to your team and a good second-in-command to your boss. You have to be all these old-fashioned things:

* Dependable
* Reliable
* Strong
* Trustworthy
* Faithful
* Loyal
* Staunch
* Dedicated
* Accountable

Boy, it's all a tall order, a tough call. But the rewards are immense. Being a manager is a fantastic job if you handle it right, abide by the rules, and play it straight.

Be a Diplomat for the Company

"Diplomacy—the art of getting people to do it your way."

Anonymous

I hope you don't have to "kiss butts" to be a diplomat for your company, but diplomat you should be. The company you work for will drive you crazy at times, and at others please you to no end. If you can stay away from the politics and backbiting that goes on in any organization, you'll be doing fine. Accept that every company has bad aspects and good aspects. Focus on the good aspects and be incredibly proud that they had the good sense to employ one of the best managers in the business—you.

Speak highly of your company wherever you go and in whatever you do. This will get back to the head office and make you even more proud, because nothing generates pride better than being proud (the opposite of a vicious circle—a kindly circle?).

If you get a complaint, accept it, tell the person you will investigate, and get back to them—and do it.

Having to be a diplomat makes you question what your company represents—and that makes you question how happy you are working for them. If it is good and you are already proud—good for you. But if you have doubts, you might have to do some soul searching before continuing. Don't throw in the towel immediately—you might be of more use on the inside, changing from there.

> "HAVING TO BE A DIPLOMAT MAKES YOU QUESTION WHAT YOUR COMPANY REPRESENTS."

Just as you would go that extra mile for a customer, find ways to go that extra mile for your company. This doesn't mean you have to be a yes-person or a lackey or a doormat. You can be strong, proud, independent, rebellious, and still be a diplomat for the company.

End Game

"Is it secret? Is it safe?"

Gandalf (Sir Ian McKellen) in *Lord of the Rings*

Okay, no more rules. This is your book. Keep it secret, keep it safe. If you don't let anyone else look at it, you'll be one step ahead without having to do anything else.

I have enjoyed being a manager immensely—am still enjoying it. It has brought me great satisfaction as well as considerable stress at times. But it has always been an adventure, always exciting.

Over the years I have discovered these fundamental rules, which I don't think you'll ever get taught at a manager's training weekend or course. These rules have sustained and kept me through many years, from a humble junior manager right up to CEO of my own company. I hope they will serve you as well.

I don't expect you to learn them all, do them all, agree with them all. But they serve as a useful starting point for conscious decision making, conscious management. What they won't do is turn you into a goody-goody.

> "IT HAS ALWAYS BEEN AN ADVENTURE, ALWAYS EXCITING."

When I was researching this book, I talked to many other managers to see what secret rules they lived by and was astounded to find a great many still lived by the "betray 'em, stab 'em in the back, claw your way to the top" school of thought. Sad, really. They were all skinny and looked stressed, haunted, and unable to relax. The others, by contrast, who live by these rules, seemed happier, more relaxed and much more at ease with themselves and with their staff—and their staff respected them and enjoyed working for them and with them. Much better.

Good luck with it all.

Acknowledgments

We are grateful to the following for permission to reproduce copyright material:

Laurence C. Jones, for an extract derived from his article "Driving Out the Fear," as featured on *www.performance-edge.com*; Marthe LaRosiliere at The Motley Fool, Inc., for use of an extract derived from Seth Jayson's article "Stocks for the Lazy Investor," as featured on *www.fool.com*; Lisa von Fircks at Kogan Page, for use of an extract derived from Lloyd King's *Test Your Creative Thinking*; Smart Technologies, Inc., for use of an extract derived from their Web site article "Be a Workplace Warrior," 2004 Effective Meetings.com/Smart Technologies, Inc., all rights reserved; SmartPros, Ltd, for use of an extract derived from Bertie Milano's article "How to be Proactive, Not Reactive," as featured on *www.finance.pro2net.com*; Catherine Faber, for use of the chorus to her song "Let It Go," Catherine Faber; Dow Jones & Co. Inc., for use of text derived from Bradley G. Richardson's CareerJournal.com article "To Move Ahead, Learn from Career Setbacks," reprinted by permission from CareerJournal.com 2004 Dow Jones & Co. Inc., all rights reserved.

In some instances we have been unable to trace the owners of copyright material, and we would appreciate any information that would enable us to do so.

Notes

Notes

Notes

Notes

Notes

Notes

Why Great Leaders Don't Take Yes for an Answer
Managing for Conflict and Consensus
BY MICHAEL A. ROBERTO

Executives hear "yes" far too often. Their status and power inhibits candid dialogue. They don't hear bad news until it's too late. They get groupthink, not reality. They think they've achieved consensus, then find their decisions undermined or derailed by colleagues who never really bought in. They become increasingly isolated; even high-risk or illegal actions can begin to go unquestioned. Inevitable? Absolutely not. In this book, Harvard Business School Professor Michael Roberto shows you how to promote honest, constructive dissent and skepticism...use it to improve your decisions...and then align your entire organization to fully support the decisions you make. Drawing on his extensive research on executive decision-making, Roberto shows how to test and probe the members of your management team...discover when "yes" means "yes" and when it doesn't...and build real, deep consensus that leads to action. Along the way, Roberto offers important new insights into managing teams, mitigating risk, promoting corporate ethics through effective governance, and much more. Your organization and your executive team have immense untapped wisdom: this book will help you tap that wisdom to the fullest.

ISBN 0131454390, © 2005, 304 pp., $29.95

In the Line of Fire
How to Handle Tough Questions... When It Counts

BY JERRY WEISSMAN

You've just been asked a brutal question. How will you respond? Will you freeze? Evade? Get defensive? No way. You'll stay completely in control. You'll win them over. *In the Line of Fire* will show you how. Author Jerry Weissman began his career crafting tough questions for CBS' Mike Wallace...then became the world's #1 coach for executives planning IPO presentations with billions of dollars at stake. This book brings together everything he's learned about answering tough questions. How to prepare. How to listen. How to answer the real question. How to avoid mistakes guaranteed to lose an audience. How to get your own message across. How to control the entire interaction. You'll learn from dozens of high-profile examples, including a remarkable, blow-by-blow photo commentary on the debate answer that destroyed a Presidency. Everyone faces tough questions. Winners handle them with skill, clarity, and grace, and Jerry Weissman has spent a lifetime helping presenters do just that. Now, you can use these lessons to your advantage.

ISBN 0131855174, © 2005, 216 pp., $24.95

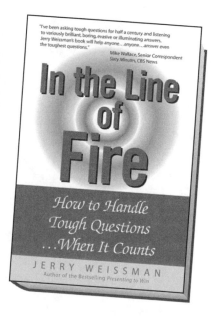

Will It Fly?
How to Know if Your New Business Idea Has Wings ... Before You Take the Leap
BY THOMAS K. MCKNIGHT

Will it fly? That's the #1 question facing everyone with a new business idea. Now, there's a systematic way to answer that question ahead of time-before you invest one dime. *Will It Fly?* introduces the Innovator's Scorecard, the first intuitive, practical tool for assessing and refining new business ideas. Created by one of the world's leading entrepreneurial consultants, this is the fastest and most confidential way to identify the strengths and weaknesses of your proposed business. Thomas McKnight's Innovator's Scorecard addresses 44 key facets of business success, from market demand to competition, pricing to management competence, finance to exit strategies. For every element, you learn what to evaluate, how important it is, how to uncover the necessary information, and how to improve their score. By answering these questions, you can fine-tune your ideas to reduce risks; protect your family and friends from losing money; quickly evaluate dozens of new ideas; and dramatically improve odds of success.

ISBN 0130462217, ©2004, 368 pp., $24.95

Clued In
How to Keep Customers Coming Back Again and Again
BY LEWIS CARBONE

Every customer has an experience with your product or brand. It can be good: it can be bad. In most businesses, however, the experience that the customer has with your product or brand is not managed in any systematic and sound way to build long-term profitability. The result is that companies lose the opportunity to leverage the value that exists in each of their customers. This is the first book that will show companies how to "engineer" the experiences of their customers, so that those customers will have a fruitful experience with your products and will want to come back

ISBN 0131015508, ©2004, 304 pp., $25.95

The Power of Impossible Thinking
Transform the Business of Your Life and the Life of Your Business
BY JERRY WIND, COLIN CROOK, AND ROBERT GUNTHER

You don't live in the real world. You live in the world inside your head. We all do. Our invisible mental models shape everything we do. Often, they keep us from seeing what's right in front of us, and prevent us from changing our companies and society...even our lives. *The Power of Impossible Thinking* is about fixing your mental models, so you can see reality and act on it. Based firmly in neuroscience, it shows how to develop new ways of seeing...understand complex environments...even how to do "mind R&D" to keep your models fresh and relevant. Whether you need to beat the competition or lose weight, your mental models may be the problem...and *The Power of Impossible Thinking* is the solution.

ISBN 0131425021, ©2005, 336 pp., $24.95

Nightly Business Report Presents Lasting Leadership
What You Can Learn from the Top 25 Business People of our Times
BY MUKUL PANDYA, ROBBIE SHELL, SUSAN WARNER, SANDEEP JUNNARKAR, AND JEFFREY BROWN

Two of the world's leaders in business knowledge and insight come together to select and profile the 25 most influential business-people of the past quarter century. The team: *Nightly Business Report*, the United States' #1 daily TV business news program, and Knowledge@Wharton, the Wharton School's online journal of research and business analysis. The book's incisive profiles show exactly how each business leader became so influential. They teach lessons you can use to discover, refine, and nurture your own leadership style—and gain powerful influence in your own career. You'll gain new insights into familiar faces (Jack Welch, Lou Gerstner, Bill Gates). But you'll also gain greater appreciation for less heralded individuals—from Mary Kay's Mary Kay Ash to Mohammed Yunus, whose 'microlending' revolution is helping millions of poor people around the world transform themselves into entrepreneurs. No other book offers this much actionable insight into this many extraordinary business leaders.

ISBN 0131531182, © 2005, 288 pp., $26.95

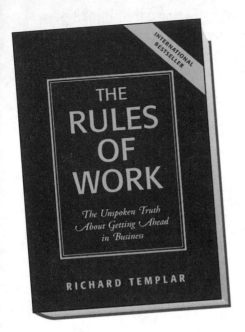

The Rules of Work
The Unspoken Truth About Getting Ahead in Business

BY RICHARD TEMPLAR

Some people seem to be just great at their job. They glide effortlessly onward and upward through all the politics, the back stabbing, the system, the nonsense that goes on. They always seem to say and do the right thing. Everybody likes them. They get pay raises and promotions. They get along with the boss. And somehow, they do all these without breaking much of a sweat or seeming to put in excess effort.

Is there something they do that we don't? Do they know something we could all learn? The answer is a most definite and resounding YES. They know *THE RULES OF WORK*.

The Rules of Work takes simple information about how people relate to each other in a completely artificial environment—the workplace—and uses it to promote your rise up the ladder of success. This is the book for you if you want to move up without becoming ruthless or unpleasant. This is the book for you if you want to be successful and still be able to live with yourself, and be regarded as a thoroughly decent person by your colleagues and bosses.

ISBN 0131858386, © 2005, 240 pp., $16.95

Strategy Bites Back
It Is Far More, and Less, than You Ever Imagined

BY HENRY MINTZBERG, BRUCE AHLSTRAND, AND JOSEPH LAMPEL

Strategy is crucial, but most strategy books take it far too seriously. Follow their advice and you'll wind up with strategies that are plodding, uncreative, boring, and doomed to failure. *Strategy Bites Back* is the antidote to conventional strategy books—and conventional strategy formation. Edited by the legendary Henry Mintzberg, it contains contributions from everyone from Gary Hamel to Napoleon Bonaparte, Michael Porter to Hans Christian Andersen: essays, poems, case studies, cartoons, whatever it takes to "free your mind" and unleash the crucial emotional side of strategy formation. Includes strategy and brinkmanship, culture, seduction...strategy lessons from your mother, from beehives, chess grandmasters, even the National Zoo. Along the way, Mintzberg, Ahlstrand, and Lampel take on the sacred cows and entrenched beliefs that keep strategists from recognizing their most powerful options. *Strategy Bites Back* doesn't just make strategy fun: it helps you define strategies that offer huge upsides and real inspiration.

ISBN 0131857770, © 2005, 304 pp., $29.95